Connecting Across Cultures

Sharing the gospel across cultural
and religious boundaries

David Claydon

ACORN PRESS

Acorn Press Ltd, Melbourne, A.B.N. 50 008 549 540
PO Box 282
Brunswick East
Vic 3057
Australia

© David Claydon, 1993
Revised edition 2000

Apart from any fair dealing for the purposes of private study, research, criticism or review, as permitted under the Copyright Act, no part may be reproduced by any process without written permission.

National Library of Australia
Cataloguing-in-Publication Data

Claydon, David
   Connecting across cultures : sharing the gospel across
      cultural and religious boundaries.
   Rev ed.
   Bibliography.
   Includes index.
   ISBN 0 908284 38 1
   1. Christianity and culture. 2. Evangelistic work.
   3. Intercultural communication. I. Title.

266

Scripture quotations in this book, unless otherwise indicated, are the author's own.

Cover: Andrew Moody, Blackburn South
Design: Ivan Smith, Communique Graphics, Surrey Hills
Printing: Openbook Publishers, Adelaide

This book first appeared as *ONLY CONNECT*. A new chapter and some new sections have been added for this revised edition and new format.

contents

Acknowledgments 4
Preface 5

Part I: **A rationale, the context and some methods**
1. Why witness 9
2. Objections to Christian witness 17
3. How the major world religions view Christianity 25
4. More than one way to witness 37
5. Not on your own 43
6. Principles for cross-cultural evangelism 51
7. Making contact 57

Part II: **The major religious groups**
8. Islam 65
9. Hinduism 83
10. Sikhism 95
11. Buddhism 99
12. Chinese religion and ancestor worship 109
13. Japanese religions 117
14. The spirituality of Australian Aborigines 125
15. Baha'i, Zoroastrianism, Jainism 131
16. Migrants with a Christian heritage 135
17. The New Age movement 141
18. Community challenges 151

Part III: **Additional Resource Units**
A. Some global comparisons and significant dates 157
B. List of countries/regions with religious groups in population 163
C. Further reading and evangelistic resources 171

Study guide 174
Index 191

acknowledgments

I want to thank all those with whom I have stayed in East Africa, the Middle East, Asia, South America and the South Pacific as well as those from Asia with whom I lived for seven years during university and post university days. They have taught me a great deal about myself and about the religions of the world.

My thanks also to my wife Robyn, whose encouragement, inspiration and example in evangelism, discipling and mentoring has greatly strengthened me in my own ministries and in sharing my understanding of cross cultural evangelism through writing *Only Connect* and this revised and extended edition.

preface

Our multi-cultural communities bring many of us into contact with people of other faiths. Many of these people are quite devout – some in fact may seem more so than ourselves! In response we may find ourselves asking questions like these:

- Can we learn something from those who follow another faith?
- Are they worshipping (being obedient to) the same God we know as revealed in Jesus Christ?
- Should we keep quiet about our own faith?
- Has the history of European wars and domination of other countries destroyed the Christian gospel in the eyes of non-Europeans?

Many are unwilling to share the good news of Jesus Christ with a person of a different cultural or religious background without first having answers to these questions. These are explored in the following chapters.

Only Connect sold out within 18 months which is indicative of the need of a book like this for everyone in a church congregation to read. The numbers of new Australians continue to grow and the presence of the world's religions in Australia is increasingly obvious. It is also estimated that in Australia's cities half the next generation will have an Asian grandparent. We are also witnessing conflicts over the right to change unused church buildings into mosques or to build new temples, and in some places those representing other religious communities seek to limit public Christian activity such as Christian ecumenical services in public schools. These are issues that Christians need to understand and know how to relate to.

Ultimately there is only one really beneficial answer and that is to share the good news of Christ's saving grace. May this book help you to find effective ways of doing this.

David Claydon

Part I

A rationale,
the context &
some methods

chapter 1

Why witness?

We are motivated to perform a task well when we have a clear idea of our purpose. In evangelism, as in any activity, the 'why' question must always come before the 'how'. There is ambivalence among some Christians about evangelism. They want to share the good news about Jesus, but they want to avoid being judgmental of other religions. In our secularised society, relativism has become orthodoxy and in what we now call *post modern* society there is a rejection of the existence of absolute truth. Those who hold this position declare that what is true for you is not necessarily true for other people. 'Your story' (for instance as to how Jesus has transformed your life) is valid, but they would state it is only valid for you. You may feel guilty of being arrogant by stating that there is only one God and only one way to him, namely the way he has provided through Jesus Christ.

Our friends and work colleagues today are accepting of people having a spiritual orientation, but they expect everyone to keep their 'spiritual' thoughts to themselves. They are tolerant of different expressions of religious ideas so long as these do not impinge on them. As a result we Christians are finding ourselves questioning whether we have the right to challenge a person of a different religious persuasion to consider Jesus.

Others will challenge us saying that family solidarity is an important value and the challenge of the gospel can be disruptive to the family. Or they will declare that multiculturalism is about 'live and let live'.

These challenges may paralyse us completely unless we go back to first principles and ask ourselves why we want to engage in evangelism at all. This chapter sets out to answer this question.

A matter of identity

If we belong to God, then we automatically represent him to the world. For Christians, witness is not an option: it flows from who we are.

Just as creation is a witness to the incredible Creator, so too we reflect to the world something about our relationship with God. The more clearly we identify ourselves with Christ, the more others are likely to see in us aspects of our faith.

God has also made it clear that all those who belong to his family are to invite others to become part of his family. For instance God called on Noah and Abraham to be witnesses to the world. Likewise the Israelites were identified by God as a people whom he had chosen to be his witnesses to the world. They were to witness to the love and the righteousness of God.

They had experienced the love of God when they were saved from slavery and they learnt through Moses about the righteous nature of God. They also knew that he is a forgiving God, but that he expected a committed response to his forgiveness. God's grace was not to be treated flippantly.

The Israelites were no different from any other nation in that they were incapable of being righteous in their own strength. God provided them with a means of forgiveness so that they might come into a relationship with him. His covenant with the people of Israel was that he would forgive them and make them his people, and that they would respond by loving and obeying him. He gave them commandments and regulations to follow, but above all, they were to reflect his holy, loving and forgiving character both as individuals and as a community. The Israelite community was to function in a distinctive way, and this would attract people of the surrounding nations to come and find out why. The prophet Isaiah summed up the challenge in these words: 'I will make you a light for the Gentiles, that you may bring salvation to the ends of the earth' (Isaiah 42:6, 49:6).

When God sent the Christ, Jesus of Nazareth, to provide the final and complete sacrifice for the forgiveness of sins, the 'children of the promise' became the new community, the church. This community was no longer identified as a particular ethnic group, but by its members' commitment to Jesus Christ as Lord and Saviour. Paul in his Sabbath sermon to the large crowd of Jews and Gentiles in Pisidian Antioch (Acts 13) quotes Isaiah 49:6, claiming that the Lord has declared the Christian community to be inheritors of the privileges and responsibilities of Israel, namely the call to be a 'light for the nations'. He expands on this theme in his letter to the Galatians and also in his letter to the Christians in Rome (particularly in Romans chapter 9).

Through Christ's work on the cross, God took the initiative to bring us back into a right relationship with him. Like the people of Israel before, we have been given a new identity by God: 'Once you were no people, but now you are God's people' (1 Peter 2:10).

The identity of Christians, both as individuals and as congregations, is determined by the fact that

- they belong to God
- they are in Christ
- they have the Holy Spirit at work in them
- they are not on their own, but are brothers and sisters in God's great family.

This God-given identity overrides that which is bestowed on us by our genetic inheritance, upbringing, cultural heritage, education, and social status. And our redeemed identity brings with it an in-built imperative to witness to God's righteous nature and saving love: we are 'God's own people that we may declare the wonderful deeds of him who has called us into his family' (1 Peter 2:9).

Note that we are not called to be religious; there is no special benefit in that. Rather God calls on us to be righteous, that is to be like him, to reflect his character (see Isaiah 42:1-9); and to tell people that there is a holy God with whom they can be in a living relationship.

As well as our identity as God's people, there are some other imperatives that motivate us to make the gospel known to others.

The Great Commission

The Great Commission is the instruction Jesus gave his disciples to take the good news to the ends of the earth: 'Therefore go and make disciples of all nations, baptising them in the name of the Father and of the Son and of the Holy Spirit and teaching them to obey everything I have commanded you. And surely I am with you always, to the very end of the age' (Matthew 28:19-20; see also Luke 24:47, John 18:18, 20:21, Mark 16:15).

Whilst the Gospel passages just referred to record possibly two or more occasions when Jesus instructed his disciples, the book of Acts records another occasion, after the resurrection and just prior to the ascension, when Jesus both commissions them to make disciples of all nations, and promises them the power of the Holy Spirit to help them carry out the task.

> *'But you will receive power when the Holy Spirit comes on you; and you will be my witnesses in Jerusalem, and in all Judaea and Samaria, and to the ends of the earth' (Acts 1:8).*

When Jesus walked the earth, most of the religions of this world were already in existence, but he did not exempt any religious or ethnic group from being told about the good news. The gospel was then, and still is today, to be taken to every people group throughout the world.

Loving Jesus

Those whom we truly love are very important to us and we wish to please them; in the case of Jesus, that means obeying him. 'If you love me, you will obey what I command' (John 14:15). The experience of Christ's love in our own lives should impel us to share this love with others both in words and in loving actions.

A changed life

We will want others to experience the radical newness of a life in Christ, one that is being actively transformed by the Holy Spirit: '...the fruit of the Spirit is love, joy, peace, patience, kindness, goodness, faithfulness, gentleness and self-control' (Galatians 5:22-23).

The great commandment

Another imperative is Christ's instruction to 'Love your neighbour as yourself' (Matthew 22:38, Mark 12:31, Luke 10:27).

In this context the word *love* means a concern for the physical, social and emotional welfare of another person. It is very likely that as we show our love in some practical way, we will also be able to share the good news of Jesus. Jesus would answer this question with his words recorded in Matthew 25: 35-36,

> 'I was hungry and you gave me food,
> I was thirsty and you gave me drink,
> I was a stranger and you welcomed me in,
> I was naked and you clothed me,
> I was sick and you visited me,
> I was in prison and you came to me.'

A matter of motivation

You may wonder if there is a question of integrity here. *Am I to show friendship to people so that I can witness to them?* No, our motivation to extend friendship is that we are God's agents in his world and so we care deeply about anyone who crosses our path. We have 'God at work in us' (Philippians 2:13) and so we are motivated by him to reflect his love. His love is both a practical concern for the welfare of others, as the Matthew 25 passage makes clear, and a longing to draw everyone to himself, to make them 'alive together with Christ' (Ephesians 2:1).

It is not helpful to think of people in categories; we are whole people and we are relating to other complete people. Loving concern for others will be for them as people, and not just for their status before God. All we do and say, as well as our motivation, is to be rooted in Christ, for 'we are his workmanship, created in Christ Jesus for good works, which God prepared beforehand, that we should walk in them' (Ephesians 2:10).

Some ask themselves, *Am I arrogant or biased in declaring Jesus as the only way to reconciliation with God?* No, our motivation comes from the enormous benefits we have experienced through having Christ at work in us and the tremendous sense of being 'at rest' in God because of the assurance of being part of his family for ever.

The first century Christians lived in a multi-religious society. The Jews believed in God as revealed through the prophets, the Romans followed mystery cults (like Mithraism), the Greeks followed other cults related to Zeus such as Artemis of the Ephesians. But filled with the infectious joy of Christ's love and motivated by his commission, the Christians witnessed through both the demonstration and the proclamation of Christ's saving love; had they not done so, there would not have been any Christians by the year AD 40!

Now that we are clear about motivation, we can go on to consider how or when one takes the opportunity to share the Good News about Jesus with another person.

A matter of sensitivity

Immigrants are faced with three major traumas:

1. They generally have come from a situation where they were part of a majority racial and/or religious group, or they were part of a persecuted minority.

   In the case of the former situation, they face the trauma of now being part of a minority and may be fearful that they will be treated with the same prejudices the minorities in their own country were treated.

   The situation is virtually the same for those who have moved from a minority context. They have come to this new country in the hope of having better opportunities, but they have inherited generations of fear and they wonder how each new person they meet here will regard them.

   Some try to cope with this fear by living as close as possible to others of their own cultural/religious background. This is what generates the tendency to the development of a ghetto.

2. They have left behind their extended family, and most immigrant groups have come from a cultural context where the extended family is enormously important. The family provides the emotional support base which we all need from time to time.

Our western nuclear family structure has robbed us of this emotional support and is one of the biggest reasons for the break-up of marriages and the breakdown of a positive value system. This extended family helps prevent negative behaviour (such as, crime, immorality, substance abuse) and often helps to hold a family together.

3. They have left behind the symbols and reinforcing environment of their cultural identity. They know that their children will grow up without these. Some desperately seek to maintain these in the home and bring their children up bi-culturally, but all see their children adopt an increasing amount of the culture of their new environment. This generates stress for the children and the parents and often for the migrant community if it has a significant presence in the area. This stress gives rise to antagonism to the adopted country, its culture and its religion.

The impact of these traumatic changes in a person's life may be coped with by some, but others are very threatened and view any attempt by 'white' people to draw them into their community or to introduce them to Christian beliefs as a form of residual imperialism, arrogance or intolerance.

Nevertheless, migrants usually want to make friends with Australians and often are interested in whether the Australian is religious. So you can share a little about your faith and you can ask your new friend about his/her faith. Comments and questions about faith can be asked quite casually whilst walking around the supermarket or enjoying a cup of coffee together. The questions can cover both what the friend believes and what the expectations are, such as, what does the person hope to gain from the religious activities (if he/she pursues any).

This will enable you both to learn something about the person, maybe something about the person's faith and hopes, and it will allow the friendship to develop, particularly if the person regards religion as important. In these ways you earn the right to speak about your faith in the living Lord.

This book will provide you with some background information. You will find you can share your faith more readily if you have a clear understanding of who God is and what he has revealed as his will for humanity. This understanding can be strengthened by learning something about the teachings of other religions.

We can also be strengthened by the realisation that the gospel can meet people of different cultural/faith backgrounds. For instance, the gospel can embrace through its love those who are poor, fearful or lonely. The gospel can empower those who have lost their dignity, identity or self esteem.

As God's people we are called to be a 'light to the people groups' (the nations) throughout the world. It is an overwhelming challenge, but the fact is that

> *'the Gospel is the power of God for salvation to everyone who has faith.' (Romans 1:16)*

Praise God that it is the gospel we are proclaiming in the power of the Holy Spirit and not ourselves! (2 Corinthians 4:5)

chapter 2

Objections to Christian witness

n the previous chapter, we reflected on God's initiative to communicate himself in a particular way for a particular reason and we saw that there is no doubt in the Scriptures as to the responsibility of the church in the world.

Some people however, are concerned as to whether God may have chosen to reveal himself in other ways to other ethnic groups. The motivation for this concern lies in the genuine desire not to appear to be judgmental of non-Christian religious ideas. There has been much discussion of this subject particularly in the past few decades. A growing awareness of the devoutness of people of other religions, and the embarrassment of two European wars in the past century initiated by a 'Christian' country, generated a deep concern as to the validity of proclaiming Christ as the global Messiah.

One indicator of how a significant part of the church universal has been reflecting on this issue is the debates at the various Assemblies of the World Council of Churches (WCC). During the decades following the First World War there was considerable debate as to whether it was necessary to make known the gospel of Jesus Christ to all the world. Then in 1982 WCC set up a study group in which some of its members and some committed evangelicals conferred. They produced a document entitled *Mission and evangelism – an ecumenical affirmation*. This document made it clear that Christ is to be announced to every people group throughout the world:

> The biblical promise of a new earth and a new heaven where love, peace and justice will prevail...invites our actions as Christians... *The church is sent into the world to call people and nations to repentance, to announce forgiveness of sin and a new beginning in relations with God and with neighbours through Jesus Christ. This evangelistic calling has a new urgency today.*[1]

The document gave a detailed comment on our call to mission and pointed out that 'Jesus Christ was in himself the complete revelation of God's love.'[2]

It argued for conversion stating that 'the proclamation of the gospel includes an invitation to recognise and accept in a personal decision the saving lordship of Christ.'[3]

And it concluded:

> The church is called to be present and to articulate the meaning of God's love in Jesus Christ for every person and every situation...The same Lord who sends his people to cross all frontiers and to enter into the most unknown territories in his name, is the one who assures [us]:
> 'I am with you always, to the close of the age.'[4]

The global gospel

Notwithstanding the 1982 affirmation of *Mission and evangelism*, some people have lingering doubts as to whether Jesus Christ is the only way to become totally and eternally reconciled with the one true God. Quite a number of books have been written attempting to show that other religions are equally valid routes to God's grace. Some of their arguments are:

- Christ could be anonymously present in all religions particularly in the form of the *logos*, the 'Word' [Raimundo Panikkar]; or
- God's grace could be at work in all religions, even though the fullest expression of God's grace is to be found in Christ [Paul Knitter]; or

- There is no compelling evidence that God meant Christ to be the only path to salvation [John Hick]; or
- The real purpose for Jesus' ministry was to demonstrate for us all such endearing values as justice, compassion, love and mercy [W. Cantwell Smith].[5]

The chief reasons for the reluctance to admit to the truth of Christ's own words that he alone is the way to the Father (John 14:6), seem to be:

1. It seems arrogant to declare to some one that, 'the understanding which I have about God is the truth and anything not in accordance with it by definition cannot be true.'

2. The other world religions have been around for so very long, except for Islam and Sikhism (both of which are derived from other religions), that surely there must be something in them which is valid, otherwise millions of people will have died without ever knowing that they were following a false route.

3. Those who are really very devout in the pursuit of their traditional religion will surely be honoured by God for this.

4. Over the centuries so few people have been converted from their traditional religion to Christianity.

5. Christianity has not lived up to the biblical expectations and has failed to be the witness it should be to the almighty, holy God revealed in the Bible.

6. Christianity has impacted upon the world religions and given them a new enthusiasm during the past hundred years. These same world religions may be able to also impact upon Christianity and sharpen its understanding of revealed truth. Therefore, Christianity needs the other religions.

The force of these arguments cannot be ignored. On the other hand, there are also some very clearly stated facts which Christians cannot simply set aside because of some nervousness about apparent arrogance or failure to be effective witnesses. These are:

1. The God who has revealed himself, through his interaction with the Israelites and the instructions to them given

through the prophets, and then in the coming of Jesus, has also called on those who know his name to make him known throughout the earth, as discussed above.

2. Christ's instructions to go into all the world to all people groups (*ethnes*) is a clear mandate, which if ignored means we are disobeying Christ.

3. If Christ is not the only 'way, the truth, the life' (John 14:6), then either he never said this and the record is incorrect, or he was deluding himself. If the former, then one can only wonder why the disciples and those in the church of the first three centuries believed this and were willing to be tortured, thrown to the lions or suffer in other dramatic ways for something they knew was or may have been false. They clearly believed that Jesus said that there was no other name by which people could be saved. If Jesus was deluding himself, then we cannot trust anything else he said and the whole of the Christian faith collapses.

4. The logic of what God has done for us in justly forgiving us is so clear in Christ's death on the cross. Remove this and we have lost divine justice. Lose divine justice and we have no objective basis for human justice.

5. Christ was not on this earth merely to demonstrate a holy life and enduring values like compassion. He came supremely to justly pay the penalty for our rebelliousness against our maker. In doing so he provided not simply an example, but an absolute measure for what really is love, is justice and is compassion. Without Christ's work on the cross, these values would have no objective meaning and each society would provide its own meaning without fear of being fairly evaluated. History has shown that Christ's work has provided humanity with the only absolute, the only anchor for declaring what is or is not human justice. Remove the absoluteness of Christ's work and the absoluteness of justice disappears.

6. If God has revealed himself in some way through every religion then we have an even more difficult task, namely to understand how a loving God would give such totally different information about himself and his expectations to each group of people. In fact, apart from Judaism and Islam,

none of the other religions claim to have a revelation from God. They are the development over a period of time of human imagination seeking to interpret life and death and the purpose of existence.

Judaism has the right to claim God's revelation, and we pray that in due course the status of Christ will be understood and accepted. Islam has drawn some of its teaching from the Old Testament and a Gospel. It has 92 references to Jesus but clearly rejects the claim of Christ as the Son of God and the Saviour. It sees itself as the final and perfect revelation of God through the prophet Mohammad. There are quite a few who have been born in a Muslim country, have studied the Qur'an and all that it has to say about Jesus and have come to their own conclusion and quietly accepted Christ as the Son of God and their personal Lord and Saviour.

7. A belief that all religions provide channels to God's saving grace, must logically cause Christians to give up the central doctrines of the Christian faith such as, the Trinity, the Incarnation and the uniqueness of Jesus Christ and his work on the cross.

8. There is another side that should be taken into account, namely *how followers of other religions* see the argument that either Christ is anonymously present or that all religions are equally valid.

Muslims would be violently against both arguments – an anonymous Christ or equal validity. To them this would be blasphemy!

Hindus object to the declaration that Christ is the only way, but they would be happy to have Christ among their plethora of divine beings. But those who have been converted from Hinduism to Christ declare that the differences are so enormous that anyone who has lived under the burden of Hindu reincarnation teaching and the consequent demand for constant *puja* (religious acts to gain merit) could not possibly think that Hinduism was an alternative route to salvation. A Hindu may be very religious, they would say, but there is no way in which through Hinduism one can acquire righteousness.

> *Buddhists* technically do not believe in the divine and regard the acceptance of Buddha's teaching to be the only route to acquiring a state of perfection. They reject Christianity as having anything useful to offer.
>
> *Jews* committed to *Judaism* continue to reject the possibility that Jesus was the long expected Messiah and so totally reject the view that Christ is anonymously present or that Christianity could be seen to be a valid alternative.

One way round these issues is to admit to the necessity of Christ's death on the cross, but to declare it as being applicable to all people in all places over all time, whether or not people know anything about Christ. Only those who clearly reject Christ would then be excluded from eternal life. This is a comforting thought, and may well be applicable for some categories of people such as those who die very young, the mentally handicapped and those about whom Paul is speaking in Romans chapters 1 and 2.

But God has not told us whether he will grant life eternally with him to those who have died without ever knowing about him as revealed in Christ. Some are certain that those who have not responded to Jesus as Saviour because they have never heard about him will be forever under judgement, for others it remains a mystery. We do know that regardless of how God will regard such people, *we* have a responsibility to take the gospel to the whole world. We are not called on to judge others or to predict their eternal destiny, but we are called on to represent Christ to the world (Matthew 28:18-20, Luke 24:44-49, Acts 1:8, Romans 10:9-17, 2 Corinthians 5:17-21).

It is not arrogance to make known what has been revealed. Dogmatism or arrogance is a description of how a person relates to another person. The Christian is called on and enabled by the Holy Spirit to be humble, to seek to learn in the very process of presenting the Gospel, and to reflect something of Christ's caring love for the person with whom one is sharing the good news.

If we fail to make Christ known, then the church would have no real purpose except to be a mutual caring society. We would in fact be disobedient to our Lord, for the church exists to be God's witnessing presence in the world. Mission must be at the very heart of the church.

Christ's Commission has made it definite that the gospel is for the whole earth. The Commission has its roots in God's redemption and calling of Israel to be a 'light to the nations'. Its substance is the crucified, risen and ascended Son of God and its energy is the dynamic presence of the Holy Spirit.

This must indeed be the dominating challenge to God's people.

1 Emphasis is as in the original – see *International Review of Mission*, Vol. LXXI No. 284 (October 1982) 427
2 ibid., p. 429
3 ibid., p. 432
4 ibid., p. 447
5 These authors have written in a number of publications. The significant ones are:
John Hick, *God and the Universe of Faiths*, 1973
John Hick, *The Myth of God Incarnate*, 1977
Paul Knitter and John Hick (eds.), The *Myth of Christian Uniqueness*, 1987
Paul F. Knitter, *No Other Name?*, 1985
Raimundo Panikkar, *The Intra-Religious Dialogue*, 1978
Karl Rahner, *Theological Investigations*, vol.5, 1966
Wilfred Cantwell Smith, 'Mission, Dialogue and God's Will For Us', in *International Review of Mission*, Vol. LXVIII: 307 (July 1988) 360-74.
A thoughtful and detailed response will be found in Lesslie Newbigin, *The Gospel in a Pluralist Society*, 1989

chapter 3

How the major world religions view Christianity

ach of the major religious groups has developed its own ideas about Christianity in response to a range of influences. In non-European countries, for example, people's view of Christianity has been influenced by

- their own religion and their cultural expectations of behaviour.

- the size and nature of the Christian church in those countries.

- the way 'white' people (whether tourists, business people, trading seaman or missionaries) have behaved in those countries.

- the dominating political and/or social ideology (system of ideas about the nature and purpose of life, the basis on which people relate to each other and so on) in the country and the extent to which this is anti-'white', anti-Christian, and/or anti-religious.

History has also been a considerable influence on outsiders' perceptions of Christianity, especially as some European 'Christian' nations have wielded a great deal of power over the other nations in recent centuries. Let us glance at the events that have had a decisive impact.

World events and the spread of the gospel

In the first few centuries after Christ was on earth, the gospel spread quickly throughout the Greek speaking Roman empire. Some of the significant reasons for this were:

1. The *Greek language* was being widely used following the establishment of the Greek empire (334-326 BC) by Alexander the Great.

2. Following the establishment of the Roman empire from 265 BC, *Roman law* was consistently and predictably applied throughout the Mediterranean countries. This enabled people to travel safely so that trade routes flourished. (The Empire began to collapse in 426 AD.)

3. The *cities* built under Greek or Roman influence were very highly developed and sophisticated. Education was highly regarded. Alexandria in Egypt, Rome and Ephesus had the three largest libraries in the world at that time. The cities had beautifully built civic and public areas, plus running water and drainage systems. These cities attracted people from throughout north Africa, west Asia and Europe. They were multi-cultural cities, providing a stimulating environment in which people felt free to question their traditions and to generate new ideas.

4. The young Christian church was characterised by a *sense of belonging*. Members cared for each other regardless of their ethnic background.

5. The young church *refused to compromise* with pagan and immoral practices. The fact that converts had to break with such cultural practices created a church membership which was totally committed to Christ and thus enthused to resist all pressures even if under the threat of persecution.

MAP 1: Alexander's Greek Empire 323 B.C.

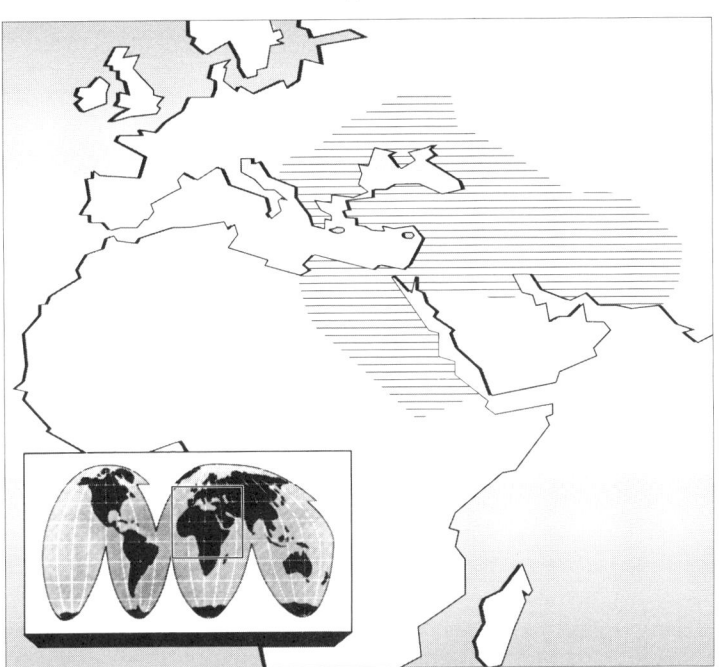

Growth under persecution

Until 313 AD, when the Emperor Constantine was converted and proclaimed freedom of worship, two and half centuries of persecution tested the quality and commitment of those early Christians. It also developed within the Christian community a sense of humility, and a reminder that like Christ we should not take the route of power but rather the way of the cross, the way of suffering (see Mark 8:34-35, John 15:18-27). Persecution arose again in some parts of west Asia and north Africa with the rise of Islam from the seventh century and again a very serious period of persecution under Tamerlane in the fourteenth century. Today many Christian communities (in the Middle East, Asia and Africa) are suffering persecution under Islam.

MAP 2: The Roman Empire 100 A.D.

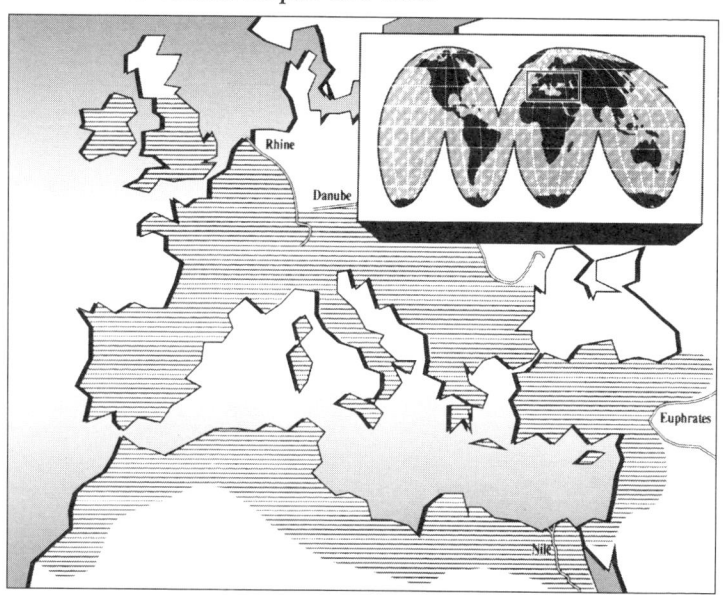

During the early centuries of persecution Christian attitudes were shaped as to how Christians are to function in this world. In particular, there has grown within the church a deep desire to express caring compassion for all in need. Furthermore, the humiliation of the cross has helped Christians to recognise that all are equal before God and that exploitation is totally against the character of God and therefore must be rejected by all who claim to belong to his family.

The way the Christian community accepted persecution and yet persisted in faith was very telling and was in itself a major witness attracting others to the faith. It is interesting that this is still so today. For instance:

> In Kaduna State, Nigeria some Muslims attacked a church after they heard that the preacher had made negative comments about Islam in the sermon. As a result three Christians and three Muslims were killed. The Muslims carried their dead on stretchers through the city of Kaduna and called out saying, 'look at what the Christians are doing to us!' As a result massive riots broke out and 120 churches were burnt

to the ground. On Sunday the Christians met in their usual place of worship and sang and listened to the word of God being taught. But now those who lived nearby or were walking by could hear the sermon and see how the people so enjoyed expressing their joy to the Lord.

On Monday it started to rain and for the next 13 weeks it rained everyday except on Sundays! Every Sunday the Christians held their service in the ruins of their church buildings. The Muslims could only marvel that this had to be the work of God and as a result many became Christians.

This does not mean that all persecution results in growth of the church or in a maturing of the Christians. Throughout the past two thousand years we have seen whole Christian communities completely wiped out of existence (e.g. in west Asia) and have seen how very difficult it is in some countries today for people to become Christians. In some places Christians have to hide their faith.

When persecution has occurred it may have kept Christians humble; it certainly has prevented people becoming Christians for the wrong reason, such as economic or political gain (generally referred to as 'rice Christians'), and the persistence of Christians through persecution has validated the power of God, ensuring that his good news would not be eradicated.

Damage to the gospel

On the other hand Christians and those seen to be Christians have sometimes behaved in ways which have done great damage to the gospel, probably far greater than that wrought by persecution. Negative perceptions of Christianity have developed as a result of the following phenomena.

Wars

Throughout the Muslim world (the Middle East, Muslim Africa and Muslim Asia) non-Christians have a greater impression of Christianity as a war-mongering religion, on account of the wars mentioned below.

The Crusades of the 11th to the 14th centuries These were military expeditions mounted by European 'Christian' rulers to the

Holy Land to protect pilgrims and to recover the Holy Land and in later years to recover Egypt and Constantinople from the Muslims. The first Crusade was 1096-99; the last in 1444. See chapter 8 for more on the crusades and Part III, section A for significant dates, noting that the Muslims started conquering vast areas within a year of Mohammad's death.

The French revolution in 1789 This was a revolt against the king and the wealthy at a time of great poverty and an uncaring government. The revolution brought into being the first known republican government.

The Napoleonic wars Napoleon Bonaparte became the military dictator of France in 1799. He had already won a war against Italy and Egypt. In the following years he held campaigns against England and most of Europe until the allies finally defeated him in 1815.

The Opium war with China In 1839 the Government of China confiscated vast quantities of opium which were being brought into the country by Britain's East India Company. Britain needed this trade and brought in gunboats to force China to accept the trade in opium.

The American Civil War This started in 1861 with a view to unifying the nation, but on 1 January 1863 the aims of the war was extended to include the abolition of slavery and continued for another two years.

The Russian revolution was in 1917 and was engineered by Lenin on the basis of Karl Marx's ideas about how to prevent exploitation of the workers.

The Spanish Civil War was in 1936 in the context of the massive problems created by the Great Depression. The ferocity of the war was due to the interference of other European powers.

The First and Second World Wars (1914-18, 1939-45) were the most devastating wars the world had ever seen. Whilst East Asia was unaffected by the First World War, the Indian subcontinent was very much aware of it and many Indian soldiers joined with the British in fighting the Axis powers. At that time some Hindu leaders took the opportunity to declare that Christianity was no different to any other world religion. They said it was a regional (ethnic) faith and therefore should not be adopted by Indians. These world embracing wars are seen by the South (the non-European, non-

North American world) as wars between Christianity; however, towards the end of the Second World War, war flared up in the Pacific – this was initiated not by the 'Christian' North but by the Japanese. The fact that there have been many regional wars since then has shown how the whole world seems to be inclined to turn to war at various times and the label of 'Christian' on war has become muted.

The history of colonialism

Particularly during the 19th century and until the mid-20th century, European powers controlled most African and South American countries and a number of Asian countries. This was the era of colonialism and imperialism.

The British colonised much of East and West Africa, the Indian subcontinent, North America, Australia and New Zealand and at the end of the First World War they took some of the Pacific Islands and Tanganyika which were German possessions at that time. The Spaniards colonised Central and South America and the Philippines. The Portuguese colonised Brazil; Angola, Mozambique and Portuguese Guinea in Africa; and a few islands like Macau, Goa and East Timor. The Dutch colonised Indonesia and Suriname in South America.

(See map 3 for details of the colonisation of Africa)

Colonial history has left an impression among the people of the South countries that Christian ('white') people are arrogant and judgmental and disrespectful of other cultures and religions. This is because the colonising powers ignored local leadership and often sought to discourage the practice of traditional customs.

Of course colonialism did not start in the 19th century. Throughout history, ethnic groups have taken control of other ethnic groups, for example the establishment of the Greek Empire; the conquest of the Greeks by the Romans; the Ottoman Empire (a Muslim regime); the Muslim-Arabic conquest of North Africa and the Moghul-Muslim conquest of parts of the Indian subcontinent. Another example is the evolution of Nepal into one country from many separate valleys through the conquest of one fiefdom (feudal estate) by another. See Part III, Section A for the dates of these events.

MAP 3: Imperialism in Africa 1914

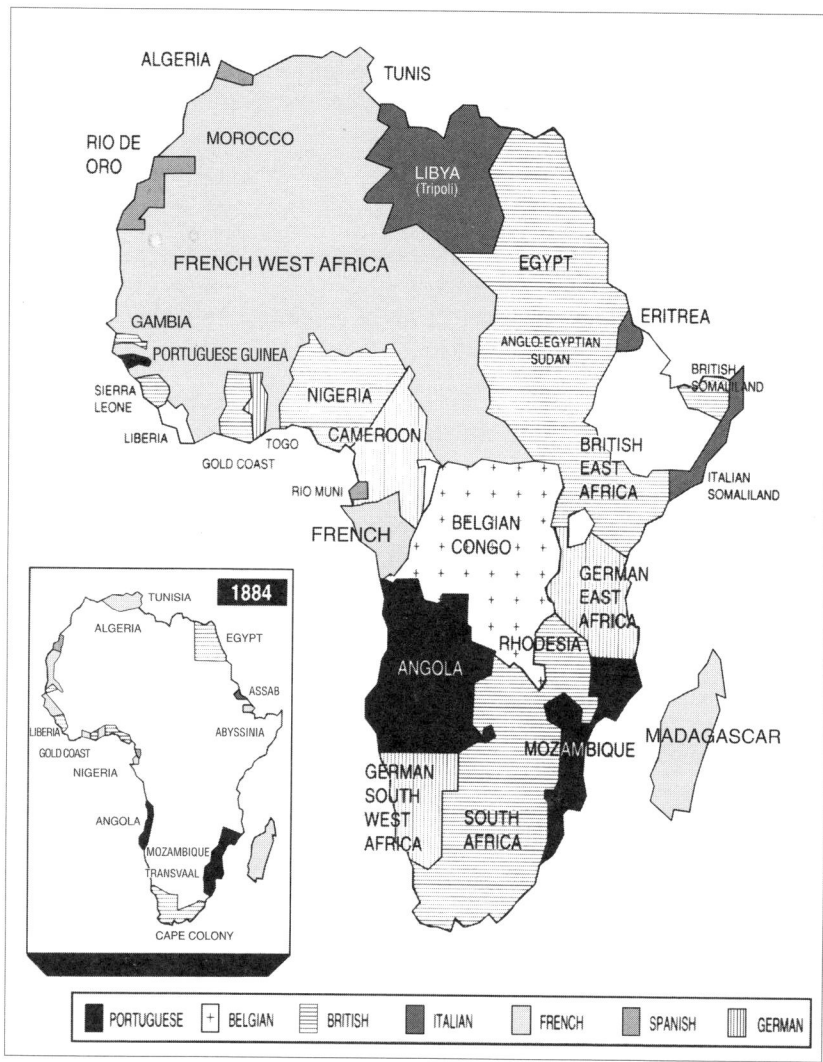

Economic exploitation

A legacy of the colonial era has been the inequality of economic relationships between the western nations (North countries) and their former colonies. For example, some of the North countries have obtained natural resources from the South countries without paying a fair price, and sold them their own products at inflated prices. A North country might send its own experts to mine a precious metal in a South country. In many situations the North country pays a low wage to miners and sells the final product at a very profitable price.

Another form of exploitation is to lend funds to a poor country but demand a rate of interest that the country cannot afford. As the interest charge remains unpaid it is added to the loan and the charges continue to grow, until the point is reached where the indebted country is using most of its resources to pay the interest. In recent years debt relief has been declared for some of these countries, but the North ('Christian') countries are still seen as being exploitative. New ways of helping countries still need to be devised.

Moral decadence

Muslims in particular, but also others in African and Asian countries, are appalled at the decadence of today's Europeans. Westerners wear clothes that attract attention to the body; and produce films, videos and internet programs in which violence, immorality and greed are often prominent. It appears that the negative values that Christians are thought to oppose are being promoted by the 'Christian' west. Positive community-developing values seem to be disappearing. Because we who live in the west are more conscious of our technological progress, standard of living and political freedom (all far ahead of those in most countries of the South), we tend to be blinded to this moral decay.

Prejudice

Migrants from South countries often find that they face a range of prejudices in their adopted countries, usually because of their dress, customs, appearance or language, but sometimes because they are also seen to be taking jobs from the locals. The migrants then have another point to make against Christians: that they do not practice what they preach, they do not demonstrate that God cares equally for all people.

Fresh demonstration of the true gospel

The witness of the nations of the North to the world about the gospel has indeed been appalling. Notwithstanding these negative facts however, Christians have done a great deal to demonstrate to the world the caring love of Christ and his offer of eternal reconciliation with the Father. For instance, Christians have in earlier centuries led the way in scientific studies (e.g. Isaac Newton, 1642-1727), in medical research (e.g. Joseph Lister, 1827-1912), and in social reforms (e.g. John Newton's campaign against slavery: first prohibition 1807). Through the modern missionary movement (started in 1792), Christians have brought health and education to lands where it was desperately needed. They have enhanced ancient cultures by a massive program of committing tribal languages to writing: the United Bible Societies have a record of over 2000 languages in which at least portions of the bible have been translated – most of which was done by missionaries assisted by local people.

Christians have also fought for the rights of indigenous people in numerous situations, e.g. the work of J.H. Oldham and others through the Conference of British Missionary Societies in 1920 to stop the exploitation of Kenyans and the Indian guest workers in Kenya.[1]

The witness of nationals

There are today Christians in every country (other than one or two Islamic States). In some places Christians have to be quiet about their faith yet they still want to hang on to their commitment to Jesus because of the joy they have found in the assurance of being part of God's eternal family. Everywhere else Christians are witnessing to the joy they have in a transformed life, to the assurance of salvation, to the gifts of the Holy Spirit in their daily lives enabling them to resist temptation, to minister to others and to worship the Lord in a deep and satisfying way.

As I have met with many Christians around the world I have had so many say to me, 'David, you will never know the contrast between following the religion of my upbringing and the freedom and certainty of belonging to Christ.' Others have said to me, 'David, my religion was so burdensome and unsatisfying, but now I have met Jesus, it has been such a joy to be in a living relationship with a loving Lord and Saviour – why don't you send out more missionaries to share this good news?'

---

1 See for instance Brian Stanley, *The Bible and the Flag*, Leicester: Apollos, 1990

chapter 4

More than one way to witness

he Bible does not tell us how we are to be witnesses to the gospel but it does make it clear *that we are* to be witnesses as we saw in chapter one. Human beings are not robots! God has made us with great capacities, the most important of which is the capacity to love others and so to develop relationships with them. God loves us and provides through Christ a way for us to respond to his love. His love should then deeply influence the sort of people we are and the priorities we have.

Paul for instance, challenged the Christians in Ephesus:

> You have been made alive in Christ...by grace you have been saved through faith, it is God's gift to you...created in Christ Jesus for good works...through his Spirit in you so that Christ dwells in you through faith...rooted and grounded in his love...and grow up in every way into Christ. (Ephesians 2:1,8,10; 3:17; 4:15)

The gospel in your own life

Everyone is a witness whenever other people are present. Our witness is not only in words, but in everything we do and the way we do it. What are we witnesses to? Most of the time we witness to some aspect of our personality; sometimes to our values (what is or is not important to us), allegiances (the X football club, our ethnic roots) or prejudices (attitudes to people who are different from us) and sometimes to our religious views.

Most of us are inadequate witnesses to the loving, forgiving Christ who is at the centre of our lives. But God knows that and he has sent his Holy Spirit to be at work in us so that we will grow up in Christ, in other words become more and more like him. Our very character can become a means by which Christ will draw someone to himself.

To keep a critical eye on the sort of persons we are and to ensure that we continue to mature in Christ we need a spiritual regimen that keeps us in touch with God. This regimen would include ideally:

- Regular gathering with fellow Christians to learn from God's word and to give him our praise;
- Regular times through the week for praying based on what has been learnt from the study of God's written word;
- Fellowship with a small group of Christians who may help us to recognise areas of our personal lives needing to be transformed and/or will encourage us in our Christian growth and service;
- Reading books which will challenge our thinking and our habits, and books about other Christians and how God has been at work in their lives.

Most of those who have been brought up in another religious tradition know very little about Christ. What they do know is usually very distorted, so they are unwilling to read about or listen to someone talk about the Christ they think of when they hear his name. The one way we can reach them is to function and relate to them in a way that is attractive and contradicts their assumptions.

The gospel in word

As discussed in chapter one, we are also called on to share in the grand task of declaring God's free gift of reconciliation. This is a specific verbal activity. As we each have different gifts, we will find different ways of making the gospel known. Some may only have the gift of responding to a question about their faith. Others will be able to take the initiative to gossip the gospel, and others will find that they can talk about Jesus as part of a structured church activity. There are a variety of ways of speaking about Christ and our church traditions may have quite an influence on what we are comfortable with.

Within Christendom there are four traditions regarding ways to witness to the gospel.

The word through liturgy

Conducting a *service of worship* (the liturgy) is in itself a witness. This tradition has its historical roots in the church of the earliest centuries. In each area, liturgies were developed as a way of providing illiterate people with a pattern of meaningful worship in which they could be involved. Learning prayers and creeds by heart was in keeping with the then normal way of remembering and passing on stories and accumulated wisdom from one generation to the next.

The declaration of one's faith by the whole congregation (and not only by some individuals out front) can be a powerful proclamation of the gospel truths.

The ceremony of remembering Christ's death and resurrection for us today (as detailed in 1 Corinthians 11 and the Gospels) and referred to variously as the Lord's Supper, the Holy Communion or the Eucharist, was and still is today presented by the Orthodox churches as a drama. As such it is more than a declaration in word, it also a declaration in life.

The only problem today is that anyone not brought up in a congregation where the liturgy has a heavy emphasis on the drama dimension, would need an interpreter to explain what is being said and done, and why. But then even a service that does not have a written liturgy usually requires some explanation for a total outsider.

This need could be met in a celebration conducted specifically as an outreach event. A joyful service in which there is a real sense of community and participation can be most attractive to an outsider; after all this is supposed to be a foretaste of our fellowship together when we are in the wonderful presence of God forever.

2. *The word through friendship*

A quite different approach is that of *friendship evangelism*. Here the emphasis is on a mutually enriching friendship between, for instance, two or three people or a group of people doing things together.

In working across cultural and religious boundaries, friendship evangelism has proven to be the most effective means, particularly where a person is prejudiced against Christianity.

Through friendship, we learn about one another's attitudes, hopes and expectations. If the friendship crosses cultural boundaries then we may learn something about each other's cultural and religious traditions. In this context of mutual interests you can with integrity declare your understanding of who God is, how he has revealed himself and the response he calls for.

This context also provides a sound basis for discipling a person. Like Christ's disciples, many will need to grow in their understanding of the gospel before they can respond to it.

On the other hand some, like the Philippian jailer (Acts 16:22-36), will respond to just one event even if there has been only a very brief outline of the gospel (e.g. a person helped at a time of need responds to the demonstration of Christ's love). But such people then need a friendship context in which to grow in their faith and to learn how to cope with the pressures (enormous for some) to return to their traditional religion or atheism. The Philippian jailer would have been very dependent in the early days on the support and teaching of those who gathered with Lydia on the river bank or in her home.

3. *The word declared*

Most of us can manage to maintain only a given number of friendships. So if friendship evangelism were the only acceptable form of evangelism, very few people would get to hear the gospel.

Even in the context of a friendship, the point must come when the gospel is specifically stated as a challenge to the hearer.

There are a number of small booklets that you can use to explain the gospel. There are also some program resources that provide more detailed approaches both to the gospel and to immediate follow-up. These are listed in Part III, Section C at the back of this book.

Special services, rallies and crusades are other ways in which people can be confronted with the claims of Christ. There is a certain objectivity about public events which makes it easier to directly present the gospel. But usually those who are there to hear the gospel are there because a friend or a neighbour has invited them to come.

Be open to the possibility that God's Holy Spirit is already at work in the other person and note that you are responsible to answer questions already taking shape in that other person's mind.

- Ask the Holy Spirit to be at work in your mind to give you the wisdom and the relevant words you need and to be at work in the will of your friend,

- Prayerfully listen to the other so as to gain an understanding as to the other person's thinking and attitudes,

- Be clear in your own mind as to what to say about the gospel when the opportunity arises, and

- Expect that God is at work through you and in the life of the other person.

4. *The word in the public arena*

Media outreach is a fourth method of communicating the Good News. Letterbox drops by Christians in the neighbourhood inviting people to an interesting type of activity (e.g. a craft event) and/or an attractive brochure about who Jesus is, can indicate to neighbours that Christians care.

Radio programs generally have quite a sizeable listening audience and are not overly expensive. Those involved in producing them need to have a good understanding of what will keep a listener listening!

A monthly full page advertisement in the local community newspaper informing people about your church and what it offers will stir some to come and 'check you out'. Often they will have some religious background long since forgotten. Your advertisement will have shown them that this church is a welcoming church. They may be in need of friendship or considering where to find real meaning in life. Remember too that migrants are often homesick and lonely.

The gospel in action

The gospel needs to be seen as well as heard. It should be evident in the life of each Christian as we discussed above, but it will be seen also in the way that the church responds to community needs and concerns. Such a response may be described as the fruit of the gospel.

For many, this fruit will create the first awareness that there are Christians in the community, or that the Christian faith is interested in (God's) creation, or that the heart of the gospel is God's love thrusting his people out into the world of need.

In each community the way in which the gospel can be demonstrated as a lively, relevant force will be enormously different. The best way forward is to get together with a group of others who are also concerned to find ways in which the fruit of the gospel can be borne in the life of your community. Whatever this activity is, pray that God will use it as a bridge to the proclamation of the gospel. We will look at some practical suggestions for outreach in the next chapter.

chapter 5

Not on your own

ven if we are on our own when witnessing, we should know that we have the prayer and support of our congregation, or at least of a group within it. To achieve this caring support within the congregation, it is necessary to design a program specifically to take into account the gifts of the members and the opportunities that exist for ministry.

The congregation needs a plan

1. The church as a congregation needs to be motivated to think *mission*. This requires a *teaching* program and congregational involvement in *planning* ways in which contact can be made with immigrants and indeed all in the community who do not know Christ (a mission program).

2. Members of the congregation need to be *trained* in one or more of the various aspects of the mission program.

3. For a mission program to be effective, it is necessary to build members up in their capacity to exercise some *pastoral care* ministry towards one another and so have the experience to care for new Christians. A pastoral care approach towards a nominal Christian at a time of need is often what the Holy Spirit uses to bring such a person into total commitment to Christ.

4. As a congregation grows in its commitment to reach out to others in the love of Christ, there will be a fresh desire to get together to _pray_. Concerted prayers for this mission program are needed including prayers for those who are running programs, and for those talking to neighbours and caring for others.

5. Once contacted, new friends can be invited to _events_ at which the gospel will be presented in a relevant way.

6. New Christians need to be _nurtured and discipled_ and be folded into the life of the congregation.

A growing church needs an integrated program which looks something like this:

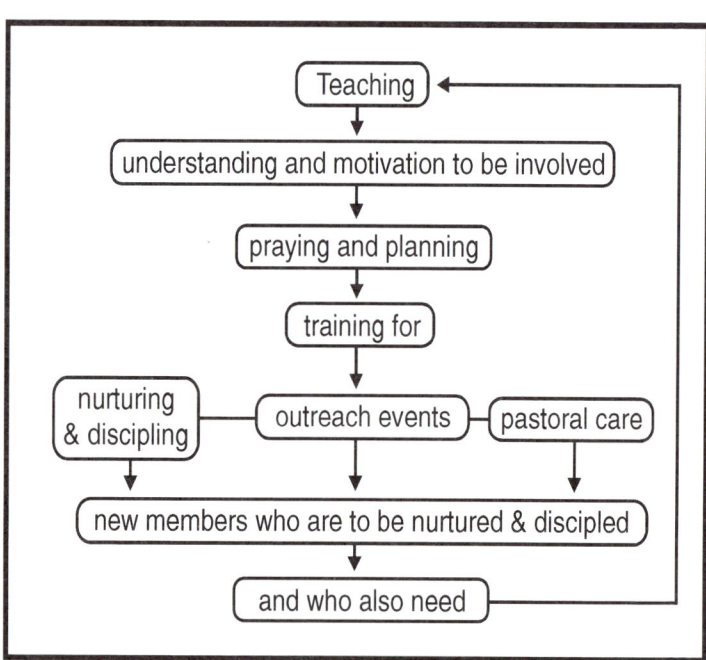

Here are some practical suggestions:

Pastoral care

Every congregation needs a program that enables members to care about one another. To achieve this you need:

- To strengthen or develop a congregational *pastoral care* network. This means training lay members in how to be involved in caring for one another both individually and in house/neighbourhood groups. Some ways of achieving this include

  - a team of people willing to take meals to homes in times of illness or emergency

  - a list of people willing to undertake practical tasks for the elderly or the poor

  - fellowship groups which meet in homes bi-monthly to get to know each other (through bible study and/or social activity such as a BBQ lunch on a Sunday) and to pray for each other

  - a list of people with some training who are willing to be with a person who has been bereaved or someone who has a long term illness.

  - training volunteer members of the congregation in basic pastoral ministry (some could be encouraged to attend pastoral care training seminars).

- To have a group of people willing to meet on a regular basis specifically to *pray* for the pastoral workers, outreach teams and any members of the congregation who ask for prayer for their home-based outreach activity.

Evangelism training

Every congregation needs a program that *enables members* to talk about Jesus to neighbours/work associates/fellow students.

- A program for training members in sharing the gospel (see Part III Section C for useful materials).

• *Attracting and caring for newcomers* •

Every congregation needs a program of services and activities that is relevant to newcomers and provides opportunities to talk about Jesus.

- A regular celebration or worship event which is attractive to outsiders.

- A specialist interest group to meet in the church complex or in your home, such as

    ❖ a craft night three times a year and invite the neighbourhood

    ❖ a play group (promote among recent immigrant young mothers)

    ❖ an after-school club for primary school children

To reach those of other nationalities, it may be helpful to conduct such activities in the home of a person of another nationality who can invite their contacts to come, or to have as a helper a person from another nationality to invite their circle of friends.

- Occasional 'contact your neighbour' activities such as a letter box drop (particularly relevant at Easter or Christmas time); or personal invitation to an activity.

- A plan for co-operation with neighbouring congregations particularly to put on

    ❖ a series of film nights on marriage enrichment

    ❖ a mock court case about some high profile local concern (a Christian viewpoint can be included)

    ❖ a musical with a Christian theme

- An occasional contact function that is in itself a valid ministry and thus a demonstration of the caring nature of the church, such as

    ❖ a coffee morning where someone explains (in appropriate languages) what government/ community welfare programs are available

- ❖ a dessert and coffee evening where someone speaks on a matter of general concern (e.g. heart disease – its causes and its prevention, understanding teenagers' struggles, preparing for and coping with retirement, a current major international political issue.)
- ❖ a film or panel of experts on relationships or some community or social issue.

As mentioned above, involving a person from another nationality means that he or she can invite contacts to these functions.

- Offer a community caring program such as emergency home assistance.

- Develop other community programs, particularly ones aimed at meeting human needs, as identified in the district, such as
    - ❖ counselling and activities for the unemployed
    - ❖ street kids
    - ❖ single parents
    - ❖ women hemmed in by language and culture.

- Organise programs for particular groups, such as
    - ❖ occasional evangelistic breakfasts to which members of the congregation can invite their new friends
    - ❖ family fun events for all newcomers to the area, such as an outing to an attractive children's fun park, or a BBQ in the church grounds with organised games
    - ❖ welcoming newcomers to the district.

A teaching program

Every congregation needs to be *taught* so that all members are clear as to the essentials of the gospel and basic Christian belief. A preaching program that aims to prepare a congregation to be involved in the witnessing life of the church could include the following units:

| *Sermon Topic* | *Bible passage* |

1. The life of the Church
   - a responsible community — Hebrews 10:19-25
   - a Spirit inspired community — Ephesians 4:1-16
   - a witnessing community — 1 Peter 2:9-10
   - a serving/caring community — Acts 6:1-7
   - a community looking forward to the coming King — James 5:7-11

2. The character of God
   - a God of Grace — Romans 3:21-26
   - a jealous God — Exodus 19:4-6; 20:1-7
   - the judge of all the earth — Psalm 9:7-8; 96; 98
   - a God of Love — 1 John 4:7-21

3. The uniqueness of Christ
   Study the book of Hebrews, or a thematic approach based on a book (see list of resources in Part III, Section C)

4. The impact of the Gospel on people's lives
   - the meaning of justification — Romans 5:1-11, Titus 3:4-8
   - the meaning of sanctification — Romans 12, Philippians 1:9-11
   - interview some parish members about the impact of being a Christian in their lives
   - a study of some chapters from Romans, such as chapters 2, 5, 8, 12.
   - the persecuted church (see Part III, Section C)

5. Being a Christian
   - the Christian's response to those in need — Matthew 25:31-46
   - the Christian and emotions — Nehemiah 1, Jonah 4
   - the Christian and conscience — Acts 10
   - the Christian and the mind — 1 Corinthians 2
   - the Christian and priorities — Luke 9:57-62
   - the Christian and the world — Hebrews 13

A congregation could also be helped to see how Christianity is viewed by those of other religious and cultural backgrounds – see chapter three and the relevant questions in the Study Guide at that back of this book.

A shorter plan would be to use each chapter in Peter O'Brien (ed), *God's Mission and Ours*, CMS 1999 as a sermon topic and the questions for the weekly bible study.

Conclusion

When the whole congregation thinks *mission* and many are involved in *pastoral care* for one another, individuals will be encouraged to see that they have a responsibility in mission -- through some part of the congregation's program, through prayer and giving and by grasping opportunities that they see.

A congregation's attitude of caring will be noticed by newcomers, and this will enable it to provide the pastoral care and love that many new Christians need because of hurts they bring with them.

chapter 6

Principles for cross-cultural evangelism

hether one is a missionary working in a foreign country or a local hoping to reach a neighbour, there is a discipline involved in gossiping the gospel. This discipline involves the following principles.

Know what you believe

Develop a good grasp of the essentials of the Christian faith. We need a clear understanding of who God is and what he has revealed as his will for humanity. We can strengthen this understanding if we also learn something about the teaching of other religions.

The gospel message is unique in a number of areas, in particular:

- God offers free reconciliation in Christ, enabling people to come into a personal relationship with the righteous Creator;

- We are accounted righteous, not because of anything we can do, but solely because Christ's work on the cross brings us true and permanent forgiveness;

- The inner work of the Holy Spirit enables us to live a transformed life that increasingly reflects the character of Christ.

These truths are central to the Christian faith. Their impact in a person's life brings joy and often a wonderful sense of peace. We need to find ways of communicating these truths that bring out their relevance and enable us to communicate our very selves.

It will help us if we grasp more fully how the gospel can meet people of different faith/cultural backgrounds. For instance, the gospel can embrace those who are poor, fearful, or lonely; it can empower those who have lost their dignity, identity or self-esteem. At the same time, the gospel can embarrass the powerful, confronting them with the reality of God and the fact that they need humility even to be able to understand their need of God's saving love.

Start where the hearer is

Firstly, find out your friend's religious background. In some cases, you can guess this, but you will only discover a person's individual response to the religious attitudes of his/her community by asking questions. You need to be as well informed as you can be about the religion your friend follows; in particular, you need to understand those underlying aspects of your friend's world view that may provide a gateway to the gospel. The better you understand the other person's ideas and hopes, as well as your own faith, the more relaxed you can be in communicating the gospel.

It is also helpful to understand something of your friend's personal circumstances. Adjusting to life in a new country is stressful and difficult, as discussed under the heading 'A matter of sensitivity' in Chapter 1.

If the person was born in Australia or came when very young and has grown up in a family committed to its cultural and religious heritage, then the person will reflect similar attitudes to the parents but have the added stress of wanting to be identified as a 'real' Australian. So get to know your friend and the stresses your friend feels.

Cover with prayer

Paul says that we are like the clay water jar, which was used in every home in his day (2 Corinthians 4:7). While the jar itself may be well made and have a pretty design on it, its purpose is not to be a work of art, but to hold water. In other words, what counts is not how we look or how gifted we are, but the fact that God has created us to carry his message.

The task of carrying God's message is a difficult one; that is why so few get involved. But God has not only called us to do this task, he has also acted to help us by sending his Holy Spirit to work in and through us (John 14:16,25; 15:26).

Of course God may choose to use us to bring someone to the point of understanding the gospel, but it is only as a result of God's work that a person will turn to Christ in repentance and faith. So we need to be in touch with God.

Pray about *who* to talk to and commit yourself to pray regularly for a particular person with whom you are in contact. Pray also that the Holy Spirit will lead you to ask the right questions at the right time and to make helpful comments, and that he will bring to your mind the most useful texts of Scripture.

There is also the matter of spiritual warfare. The 18th century Enlightenment (a European development of ideas about nature, reason, happiness, progress and liberty) has deeply influenced the western mind. As a result we will believe only what can be proven by scientific means or clear logic. However, in recent years there has been a shift away from this logical approach and the western mind is increasingly thinking in terms of people's stories and not expecting a logical, universally applicable truth to emerge. In fact there should not be a universally applicable truth – everyone can simply believe in whatever her/his experience indicates is appropriate. This western development is not evident in South countries. Muslims are quite clear as to what is a fixed and unchangeable truth. Other religions are generally accepting of all religious ideas and so in this sense do reflect (and have always reflected) what is the current western way of thinking.

Both the older theory of logical proof and the current idea that everyone's story is valid for each person prevents people from recognising the fact of evil and the reality of the Evil One.

We need to be aware of the work of the Evil One in seeking to prevent us from witnessing effectively to anyone. We need to pray daily for the powerful work of God the Holy Spirit in our lives, asking for wisdom and strength and for protection from Satan.

Some followers of other religions are in the grip of evil powers. Pray for the Holy Spirit to be mightily at work in the person with whom you are talking, asking that the grip of evil on them will be broken.

Have a spirit of humility

As we think about taking the gospel across cultural and religious boundaries, we need to be clear about the need for a humble approach. The friends with whom we hope to share the good news have probably had a religious upbringing of some kind. With our Christian upbringing we will never be able to comprehend how those brought up in another religious context will feel about the challenge of the gospel.

Many Muslims, Hindus and Buddhists who were converted to Christianity have indicated that they were not unhappy about their upbringing as it prepared them for the full and final revelation of the one true God in Christ. Often they have an appreciation of the gospel that is lacking in people brought up as Christians.

Having a spirit of humility means that we do not need to be confrontational in our methods – we can relax and allow the gospel message to confront the hearer. Our task is simply to develop a context in which the other person can hear the message; if that is to happen we must demonstrate the caring love of God in the very way we talk and listen.

Be willing to listen

All religious beliefs touch not only on a person's thinking but also the feeling level. Often it is the symbolism, the traditional rituals and festivals that touch the feelings quite deeply. Invite the other person to share heart-felt hopes and ideas about the divine; these provide a bridge for you to talk about the revelation of God in Jesus Christ.

Listening to the other and then explaining your knowledge of God as revealed in the Scriptures, then listening to the other person again is a process that is often called *dialogue*. Dialogue does not mean a half-hearted attempt to discuss the gospel; it means genuine listening on both sides. Such listening, which provides greater understanding of the other person's thoughts, hopes, goals, hurts and knowledge of God, is a way of showing respect for that person's position and integrity. To show such respect demonstrates the caring love of God; and to go on to share what you know about Christ's love as you have experienced it is in no way a violation of this respect.

Theologian Jürgen Moltmann has said that true dialogue takes place when each person presents what is unique about his/her understanding of God.[1] It should not be merely an attempt to find common ground, although this can help the two people understand one another better.

Communication is ideally a cycle in which you listen again after talking to check for understanding on both sides. New information gained modifies the approach, making for more effective communication.

Another important part of listening well is attention to the other person's body language which, as much as the words spoken, tells you what she/he is feeling. Maintain eye contact and note the other person's movements. Your body language matters too; it is preferable to sit alongside the other person rather than sitting opposite, which can appear confrontational. We can be relaxed in the dialogue process, since we are not communicating ourselves, but the message. During every conversation be prayerfully aware that it is the Holy Spirit who will apply the message to your hearer's heart and mind.

---

1 Stated in a lecture at Vancouver in 1989.

chapter 7

Making contact

Making friends

In chapter 5, I suggested ways your church can develop opportunities for making contact with people of other faiths. Now you need to work out ways to make friends with individuals so that you can invite them to the church contact events. For instance:

- If you are a parent and you work in the school tuckshop, you could make friends with others and follow up with an invitation to have a cup of coffee afterwards.

- At a community activity e.g. the local school fête, community art show, shows in the shopping mall, municipal fireworks night, one may meet people who live only a few streets away. Follow up this contact by inviting them or their children, if they are of similar age to yours, to your home.

- Sporting clubs provide opportunities for making new friends.

- The first contact with people of other faith/cultural backgrounds is first to meet them at their point of need.

Offer to assist a new family in your street with English language conversational practice; provide information about local community services, or take a meal around in times of illness (be careful, as they may not eat certain meats and are unlikely to appreciate salads). These are all ways of both sharing friendship and witnessing to a God of love.

Having made contact, one needs to develop a friendship by listening to the other person, and looking for some common interests. One way to get a conversation going is to refer to a current event e.g. a story in the news or a Christian (or other religious) festival. There is no need to rush the conversation. Take time to explore areas of interest.

As you get to know the person, make sure that you respect the cultural expectations of polite behaviour. These vary for each religious group – see the sections 'Cultural do's and don'ts' and 'Becoming a Christian' in chapters 8 to 15.

One-to-one conversation: a suggested approach

Some people have argued that the word of God is powerful enough to bring about salvation regardless of the way it is presented or to whom it is presented. Indeed many have come to Christ through reading a small portion of the Scriptures or through hearing just a small part of the gospel message preached. Clearly the Holy Spirit can and does use us, with all our limitations, to communicate the word of God to others. But this is no excuse for laziness on our part! In most cases we will need to make the gospel message relevant to our friends when talking with them. The rest of this chapter looks at an approach to one-to-one conversation in which you seek to find points of contact between your beliefs and those of your friend, as a way of helping your friend understand the gospel and its relevance.

Introducing the question of faith

How and when do we take the opportunity to share the good news about Jesus?

It is best to use general terms in your first discussion. If you start by referring to Jesus you are likely to set up a confrontation before you know anything about the person. If, on the other hand, you refer to God, you open the way for the person to indicate his or her belief (or lack of belief) in God if so inclined.

If your friend is not an atheist (someone who believes there is no God), then you know that your friend has an awareness of the Divine – a power greater than all human power – and accepts that there is an existence beyond this earthly life. Such a person, even if possessing distorted beliefs, is already well ahead of the atheist.

The next step is to find out about the person's faith by asking questions. You can ask these questions quite casually while enjoying a cup of coffee together. Ask what beliefs your friend holds and what he or she hopes to gain from pursuing religious activities (if this is so). This way you learn something about the person. Allow the friendship to develop, particularly if the person regards religion as important, and earn the right to speak about your own faith. Do not expect to achieve much in any one conversation. Take time to listen by asking questions. Answer questions briefly, leaving an opening for the person to come back to you with a further question.

If you are aware of the declared beliefs of the religion that your friend follows, you can move far more quickly to establish a friendship based from the start on an openness to explore divine truth.

Digging deeper

Once you understand something of your friend's beliefs, you can try to draw attention to the more fundamental, perhaps unacknowledged truths that underlie them. For instance, underlying the Hindu belief in the divine is an acknowledgment that humans cannot create nature or human life; nor can they change their caste status. There must, therefore, be some force at work that is far greater than any individual or group of people.

Another example is the Confucian teaching on ancestor worship. While Confucius taught reverence for elders, whether dead or alive, partly to take people's minds off spirit worship, it was also a way of promoting positive values. The underlying belief here is that there is a righteous Supreme Being who cannot be known, and that respect for elders is representative of respect for this being.

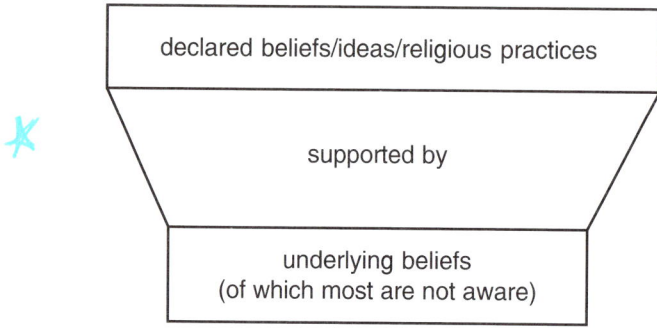

such as

- there is a power/being beyond creation
- death could not be the end of personal existence
- there is a common code of human behaviour which respects the dignity of other humans and creation

It is this acknowledgment of an unknown powerful reality that can provide the basis for a helpful positive discussion. After listening, you can explain why this powerful force must be the Creator God who has revealed himself through the prophets of Israel and in Christ Jesus.

What about the Christian's underlying beliefs? When we think it through, we can see that the Christian beliefs are based on God's general revelation in nature, and on his special revelation through the prophets, through Jesus Christ and through the written word of God.

Even if your friend is an atheist, that is, believes that there is no divine being, there will still be underlying beliefs, for example:

- human beings control their own destiny

- life has no particular value

- the body is just meat and one can do what we like with it

- right action is that which does not hurt anyone else

You can draw out and discuss these beliefs so as to bring the person to reflect on the reasons for living. For instance, if your friend believes that people can choose to control their own destiny, you could agree that we all can make choices, but we do so within some limits. We cannot choose the context into which we are born; we usually do not choose to have a serious illness or accident – and we have no power over death.

This response of yours may result in further comment from your friend revealing perhaps a belief in an unknown force, in luck or in fate. Whatever term your friend uses, it reveals a belief in something greater than oneself. This provides you with an opening to talk about the One who is greater than all creation, who does allow us to make choices, but who also wants to help us make the best choices. He will do this for all who make the most fundamental choice, namely to accept his free gift of forgiveness – forgiveness for treating God as if he did not exist – and so become a member of his family.

Alternatively, explore your friend's work or other interests and watch out for something that provides an entry point to talk about the existence of God. For instance, your friend might say, 'My boss is a racist.' You could reply, 'When I was a teenager at school we used to pick on anything that was different about another student and laugh at that person. I guess this made us feel that we were better than that other person and maybe it made us feel important. But then when I realised that God created everyone, I started to realise that we are all equal before God, no matter what our appearance or abilities. Letting God come into my life totally changed the way I saw other people.'

You would then allow time for your friend to reply, and be ready to take the conversation further into this area of underlying beliefs.

Initially your witness is most powerful, not in your words but in the way you live. Your friend or neighbour of another faith will be more impressed by the kind of person you are than with what you have to say. If you have a warm gentle approach, your friend will be drawn to you, will be open to what it is that makes you that way and will readily listen to you. Ultimately your friend needs to hear the truths of the gospel. Your witness in being the person you are is thus a bridge for conveying the word of the gospel.

Part II

The major religious groups

chapter 8

Islam

sually the word *Muslim* (one who submits to the God of Islam) is used to refer to *people*, while *Islam* means the *religion or its teachings*.

How Muslims view Christians

Muslims gain their view of Christians from two sources: the Qur'an, and contact with Christians.

The Qur'an

The Qur'an (sometimes spelt *Koran*) is the Muslim Holy Book containing what the Prophet Mohammad said was God's revelation to him and, through him, to the world. Muslims hold dearly to the teachings of the Qur'an; so the more one knows what it teaches, the greater is the scope for thoughtful conversation with them.

Muslims are taught that where there is an apparent discrepancy between one passage and another in the Qur'an, then the later revelation abrogates or overrules the earlier passage (the technical Arabic word for this is *naskh*. Reference in the Qur'an: 2:100; 13:39; 16:101; 22:52). With this understanding, it is clear to a Muslim that as the Qur'an came after the New Testament, its teachings abrogate any inconsistencies with what the Gospels teach about Jesus. Likewise, they believe that the Gospels abrogate the revelation of the Old Testament.

Muslims interpret Jesus' words to his disciples, 'I will send you another comforter...' as a prophecy of the coming of Mohammad. (Comforter and counsellor are two translations of the Greek *paraclete* which means one who draws alongside – see John 14:15-17, 25-27; 15:26; 16:7.) Some Muslims also see the question put to John the Baptist, '...Are you the prophet?' (John 1:21) as referring to Mohammad, particularly as John replied, 'No'. They confuse John with Christ at this point and believe that Mohammad was God's final messenger to the world. They see the progression of God's revelation in this way:

God revealed himself through Abraham (with the promise of being the father of a people (an *ethne*) whom God would use to reveal himself and his purposes to the world); then through Moses (with a declaration of God's covenant through the laws and the regulations); then through Jesus (with a message of discipline and commitment); and finally and completely, through Mohammad.

Those who ignore Mohammad have, in the understanding of a Muslim, stopped short of God's complete and final revelation.

Mohammad learnt about God through two Jewish tribes and two Nestorian Christian tribes who lived in and near Medina and through monks living in the Syrian desert. Muslims believe that God gave Mohammad all the sayings which after his death were collected into one volume and called the Qur'an (which virtually means to recite, since these are God's words which Mohammad was commanded to recite to the people).

Parts of the Old Testament will be found in the Qur'an. Where there is a difference, Muslims say that the Christians corrupted the text and that the Qur'an Arabic text is perfect. The Qur'an makes reference to the first five books of the Old Testament (the Pentateuch, *taurat* in Arabic), the Psalms of David (*zabur*) and the gospel (*injil*) of Jesus. There are 92 references to Jesus (*Isa*).

Contacts between Muslims and Christians

The *first* significant contact Muslims had with Christians after Mohammad died, was when the Muslims decided to take their religion to the known world. The strategy was to conquer city by city and bring the people into subjection to their new Arabian (Muslim) masters by promising good government and assuring the people that they, the Muslims did have God's final revelation. Those who refused to accept Islam were allowed to continue their Christian practices, but both the individuals and the churches had to pay heavy taxes (*jaziya*). Those who wanted to oppose Islam were warned that the penalty would be death.

During the period that Islam swept through North Africa, Christendom was divided, particularly over the Arian controversy (this was a dispute about the person of Christ whether he was both fully God and fully man). The different factions were imprisoning each other and consuming much energy in debate instead of evangelism and building the Christian community's understanding of their faith. So the Muslims concluded that the Christians did not really know what they believed, particularly about God and who Jesus really was.

The *second* significant contact Muslims had with Christians was when European Christian rulers mounted military expeditions (Crusades) to the Holy Land to protect pilgrims and to recover the Holy City and in later years to recover Egypt and Constantinople from the Muslims.[1] The first Crusade was in 1098. This was successful, but Saladin reconquered Jerusalem in 1187 and it later became part of the Ottoman (Turkish) Empire.[2]

Muslims, particularly those of Arabia and North Africa have never forgotten the Crusades and they continue to see Christians as violent aggressors, even though it was the Muslims who some centuries earlier had invaded the countries that the Crusades sought to recapture. It is of interest that St Francis of Assisi went to Egypt in 1219 and talked to the Christian and Muslim leaders to try and bring to an end the Fifth Crusade (aimed at recapturing Egypt which had fallen to the Muslims in the seventh century).

The *third* significant contact between Muslims and Christians was through colonialism. It was the Muslim Turks who first colonised a major part of Europe, West Asia and North Africa.

Following the decline of the Mongol influence, the various communities of West Asia (Asia Minor) pursued their own tribal goals. Then in 1326, Orhan, son of Osman conquered Bursa and made it the first capital of the Ottoman Empire. This Empire continued to extend itself in all directions and on 29 May 1453 Constantinople, the Christian Byzantine capital since the days of the first ever Christian Roman Emperor (Constantine), fell to Mehmet II. The famous Santa Sophia Orthodox Cathedral and all the other churches in that great city were turned into mosques and Christianity was brutally suppressed.

This Ottoman Empire continued to grow and by the mid seventeenth century, Islam had spread to the areas shown in map 4.

This empire started to break up in the nineteenth century and finally came to an end with the First World War. It had lasted four and half centuries. But by 1918, only Turkey, as we know it today was left intact.

During the period of disintegration, the Armenians, who were all Christians and had been part of the Ottoman empire, saw thousands of their number massacred, particularly on two occasions: in 1894 by the Kurds and in 1917 by the Turks.

Following the First World War, Russia, Britain and France took control over various parts of the former Ottoman Empire under various treaties and carved up other parts into new States, such as Palestine, Jordan and Kuwait. This control was seen by Muslims as a modern form of economic colonialism.

While Muslims are aware of the modern twentieth century colonial period, they seem not to know much about the atrocities of the Ottoman Empire. They believe it was a benevolent empire, whereas they saw the twentieth century powers as dividing up the Middle East in ways that would protect European interests.

The tragedies since then of the Palestinian people (1947 to the present), the civil war in Lebanon (1978-89), the Iran-Iraq war (1980-88) and the invasion of Kuwait (1990-91) are seen as a consequence of the division of the Ottoman empire by 'Christian' Europe. (During the time of the Crusades all Christians were seen to be Europeans, so Muslims came to regard all white people as Christians. In addition world events since World War II caused Muslims to view America as the foremost world power and enemy of Islam.)

MAP 4: The Islamic World Around 1650 A.D.

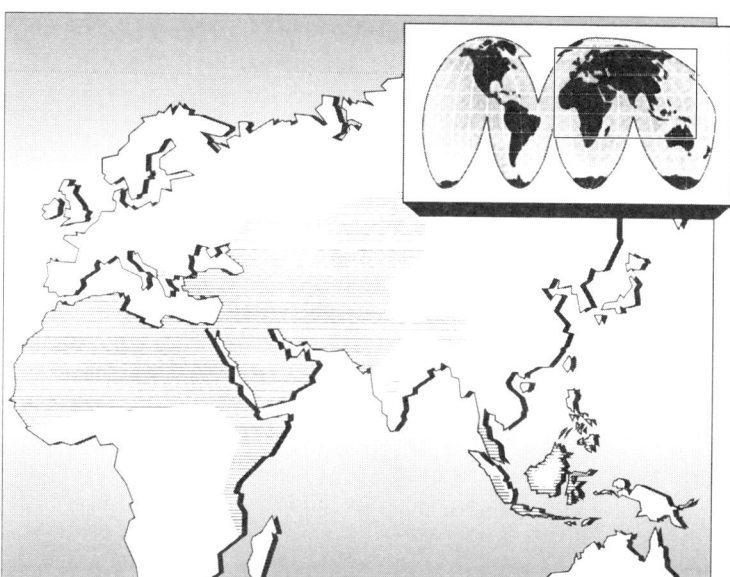

The *fourth* significant contact between Muslims and Christians arose after the Second World War with the discovery of oil in many Muslim lands (Arabia, Libya and Brunei). The British, the French and the Americans, it is maintained, manoeuvred political alignments and manipulated the markets so as to ensure a steady flow of oil, and these oil producing countries have become rich on their sales to the 'west'.

During the 1970's the oil producing countries got together in a cooperative (OPEC) and set world prices. This boosted not only their income but also their pride: at long last, after a thousand years, the Muslim world was gaining for itself some self respect. OPEC became a force in world politics and so long as OPEC nations could agree on an inflated price they could hold the Europe/American (i.e. 'Christian') world in an economic vice.

The *fifth* really significant involvement with Christians was the Gulf War of January-February 1991. This was a little more complex, since Saudi Arabia invited America and the rest of the world to protect it from a flow-on Iraqi invasion and the Kuwaiti Emir wanted help to regain control over his sheikhdom. Most Arabic nations joined the coalition forces. In Pakistan and North Africa there were some protests against the Christian west for fighting against Iraq, for what they believed was only to protect the flow of oil to the west. After all, where was the action against Israel for taking the Palestinian West Bank and their total disregard for the United Nations resolutions?

For these and many individual Muslims around the world, the Gulf War was another display of the power grabbing nature of the Christian world.

Notwithstanding this, in the Middle East countries themselves there was a new appreciation for Christians because of the enormous effort they put into caring for refugees regardless of their religious affiliation. Even in Iran, it was the Christian Armenians (who had suffered so horribly at the hands of the Muslim Kurds ninety years previously) who cared for the Kurds as they poured across that border to get away from Saddam Hussein. In Jordan it was the Palestinian/Jordanian Christians who worked so hard to help the million refugees from Iraq and Kuwait in the first few weeks of the war; later King Hussein, publicly thanked the Christians for their efforts to help the Muslims escaping from the war.

The *sixth* area of contact with the 'Christian' western world is the commercial, media and tourist contacts of recent decades. This contact has highlighted for Muslims how immoral the 'Christian' west is.

More than a set of religious beliefs, Islam is a total way of life. The Shari'a Law (the Islamic religious code of law) spells out a quite detailed behavioural code not dissimilar to that of Christians in the eighteenth century. It is drawn from the Qur'an, the *Hadith* (the teachings and practice of the Prophet as enshrined in the traditions) and the discussions of the elders such that it is difficult to be sure about some aspects of it. The criminal part of the code is clear and includes:

- no drinking of alcoholic beverages
- no sexual contact outside specific arrangements
- no man should look at a woman who is not his wife. Hence the woman needs to be covered up whenever venturing into a public place.

- within the home, women will retreat to their quarters whenever men come to the home
- there should be no pictures or images of humans or the human body (as this is seen as breaking the first commandment given to Moses and recorded in Exodus 20)
- no interest should be charged or given on loans as this hurts the poor and encourages profiteering (see also Deuteronomy 15, Proverbs 28 and many other instructions about caring for the poor in both the Old and New Testaments).

In contrast the western, 'Christian' world is seen as actively promoting drug abuse, sexual amusement and profiteering. Yet as Professor Seyyed Nasr has pointed out,

> 'The appreciation of the spiritual nature of Christian morality is especially evident where Muslims live near pious Christians. In lands such as Syria and Egypt...there was hardly a devout Muslim who did not revere and deeply respect some pious Christian friend or neighbour.'[3]

Some teachings of the Qur'an which Christians should know

Muslims treat the Qur'an with great respect. It is always placed on top of other things. Often it will be wrapped in a special cloth and will be touched only after ceremonial washing. The ideal is to know it by heart in the Arabic language. A person who knows it by heart is given the title *hafiz* (= someone who knows).

Most importantly, Muslims venerate the Qur'an because it contains the Law (as does the Old Testament). This Law (*Shari'a*) does not appear in the Qur'an in any codified way. Islamic scholars have studied the Qur'an and the *Hadith* and have developed a code of law. This law is central to the mind-set of the Muslim.

The law requires that five functions be performed by every Muslim. These are:

1. To daily declare that there is no God but one God and that Mohammad is his Prophet (the Apostle of God)

2. To pray five times a day

3. Almsgiving – helping those in need

4. To fast during the month of Ramadan

5. To once in a lifetime go on a pilgrimage to Mecca, if possible.

These five pillars of Islam are seen as essential activities in the worshipping life of the community.

Muslims believe that Jesus is the most important prophet after all the other prophets and that he led the way for Mohammad. They know that Jesus was born of the Virgin Mary and that he healed people, but they cannot believe that God would allow a prophet of his to die on the cross. As God is all powerful, they maintain he would be able to and did save Jesus from death and took Jesus to be with him in Heaven (as he did with Enoch).

Mary is the only woman mentioned by name in the Qur'an. She is identified as the mother of Jesus, the most blessed of women who accompanies the soul of blessed women to paradise.

Since the Qur'an is a further revelation following the Old and then the New Testament, both Jews and Christians are respected by the Qur'an and are referred to as 'people of the Book' (*ahl al-kitab*), references in the Qur'an are 1:7; 2:40,62,97,102,109, etc. The Qur'an is also critical of Christians and Jews for not recognising that God's final revelation has come in Mohammad (just as Christians are critical of Jews for not recognising the Messiah). The *Hadith* (written traditions concerning Mohammad's teaching and practice) outlines a range of restrictions which must be placed on Jews and Christians which virtually makes them slaves in an Islamic society.

The Qur'an categorically insists on the 'oneness' of the Divine such that there cannot be 'three persons in one', and hence they totally reject the possibility of a Triune God. If there is no Triune God, then it is impossible to accept the idea of God descending into his own creation, and hence Muslims totally reject the incarnation.

The Qur'an states that Christians believe in three Gods – Mary, who gave birth to Jesus, Jesus himself and God the Father (references in the Qur'an 3:45-51; 4:171; 5:17, 73; 9:30-31; 43:57-64). The Qur'an says that Jesus was born to Mary and that the Angel Gabriel was the one who caused this to happen. This reference to the Angel Gabriel is about as close as the Qur'an gets to the idea of God the Holy Spirit. Although there are some references to the Spirit (*Ruh*: the Breath of God), these are not developed and few Muslims would have any understanding of the Holy Spirit in the way that Christians are taught.

The Qur'an teaches that everyone is born into the world without sin. Therefore, everyone is pure and can remain good by obeying the law. A person who disobeys a law can balance this out by doing good, such as charitable works. God in his mercy will count the good against the bad. A visit to Mecca (the *Haj*) will offset most if not all of the sins a person has committed. Death in the pursuit of a holy war (a *jihad*) will result in the person going directly to heaven. However, belief in another God other than Allah is unforgivable because it means a total break in the relationship with Allah.

Since the Qur'an states that Jesus never died, it rejects the fact that Jesus paid the ultimate penalty for sin (reference in the Qur'an 4:154-158). Hence the fact of Christ's resurrection from death is also rejected. Thus the Biblical teaching about justification (being justly forgiven), sanctification (growing to be Christ-like) and grace, summed up in Isaiah by the term 'the Suffering Servant' and in the NT by the 'way of the cross' is unknown to the Islamic mind.

The rejection of the cross results in the absence of the Biblical emphasis on sacrificial love (*agape*) and on humility, and gives law an almost supreme position in determining people's relationship with God.

Groups within Islam

Islam, like every religion embraces a range of religious attitudes and teaching. For instance, there are a number of different 'denominational' groups and sects, the largest of which is the Sunnis and the Shia's are the next most significant.

Another range of attitudes that crosses the denominational/sect boundaries is as follows:

The intellectuals

Within every type of Islamic group, there are those who are well educated and who enjoy the careful study of the Qur'an and the Hadith. They seek to integrate their understanding of their faith with every day living and the demands of a political State. They are usually accepting of those of other faiths. They feel secure in their own faith and so are open to a dialogue with those of other Faiths. Many of the Sunni Mullahs and many academics are of this ilk.

The legalists

All Muslims believe that there is one sovereign God and therefore there is one law. This law includes the government of the State as well as the behaviour of individuals. Although as mentioned above the Shari'a law is drawn from the Qur'an and the Hadith together with the discussion and consensus of the elders, nevertheless, it is clear that what is stated in the Qur'an is absolute. Furthermore, since the Qur'an (in its original Arabic language: the language of God and thus the language in which it was delivered to Mohammad) is seen to be the actual words of God, all Muslims are expected to believe in its literal understanding.

Out of this position has developed a strong legal approach which embraces all aspects of life. Faith is not being fully practised unless a person lives in a truly Islamic society where Islamic laws and economic principles are applied. Those who espouse this legalist position are generally referred to by the Western world as 'fundamentalists'. But this term is not accepted by Muslims. They assume that all Muslims would hold to the position of reading the Qur'an literally.

The legalists/fundamentalists have little or no understanding of the grace of God. They do believe in the mercy of God, but only in the sense that God will offset people's good deeds against their evil deeds.

Muslim folk religion

Within each of the various denominations/sects of Islam there are those who have inherited the beliefs of their forbears, that is from their pre-Islamic days. Prior to Judaism, Christianity and Islam most people of the globe developed their own religious ideas and practices, in an interpretation of the natural features and events of their environment. An animal, a large rock, a volcano, a thunderstorm or a flood were regarded as being invested with a spirit, which needed to be recognised in some special way for the prosperity and protection of the community. This is generally known as animism.

In many situations (usually among uneducated rural people), people accepted Islam for survival reasons, but did not entirely discard their animistic beliefs. The tenets of Islam have not been well taught to the illiterate, so these people continue to have an animistic interpretation of natural events. They also turn to occult practices to divine (explain) what lies behind a particular event or to seek protection from future calamities.

There are *piers* who act like priests to provide information for a price or to cast a spell of evil on a person. The people use amulets (bracelets) to ward off evil spirits and pursue a variety of practices to protect themselves from evil and in particular 'the Evil Eye'. The saddest aspect of this folk religion is the tremendous cloud of fear under which these people live.

The challenge of Islam

Many Muslims are strict about their code of behaviour and all are strong about the need to make the Islamic faith known to those who are not Muslims. In contrast, Christians appear to be uncertain about their faith, slow to witness to it and unable to keep the commandments.

Muslims also cannot understand the tendency for Christians to keep their faith to their private life. Islam, like Marxism in the past, sees itself as valid only when it allies its teachings with political power. It demands that the law of the land be the Shari'a law and that government be led by committed Muslims who are passing laws in line with Islamic teaching. Even in countries not traditionally Muslim, the Islamic leadership will argue for the enactment of Shari'a law, at least for their own community.

Christians need to take this as a challenge not to limit their faith to personal life and to find ways to apply the truths of the gospel to the public arena. On the other hand, Christians do not look to establish the Kingdom of God on earth, and the motif of the 'way of the cross' should dominate the way Christians function in community life.

Cultural do's and don'ts

- Be friendly and natural. Just as Christ came into our world with all the limitations this placed on him, so too we need to try and enter at least a little into the world of Muslims before discussing our faith. So be prepared to join in things foreign to you such as a wedding festival.

- Muslims do not eat pork and pork products and most do not like to eat out of a utensil which has been used for pork. Christians inviting Muslims into the home for meals should have no pork in the house and declare it a 'pork free home'. Alternatively invite a Muslim friend in to morning or afternoon tea.

- Muslims do not drink alcohol.

- Muslims regard the Qur'an and the Bible as holy books and they have pride of place in the home.

- Do not denigrate the Qur'an, even by saying that it is not correct on some point of theology. You can be clear about what you know from the Bible and from experience without judging a book about which you know little.

- During the festival of *Ramadan*, Muslims do not eat or drink from sunrise to sunset, and they often appreciate a Christian neighbour who is discreet about eating at this time (e.g. not have a BBQ in the garden during daylight hours). They enjoy having friends in for their feast at the conclusion of the festival and would accept an offer of a meal in a Christian neighbour's home at some other time in the year.

- Normally in a Muslim home it is inappropriate to be dressed in such a way that arms and legs are uncovered. Only befriend a person of the same gender.

Becoming a Christian

Stumbling blocks to becoming a Christian are:

- The failure of Christians to follow the teaching of the Bible. This includes the failure to lead a holy life, or in other words, the failure to be like Christ.

- The strong family bonding which makes it a dreadful act to turn one's back both on Islamic teaching (this act is seen to be blasphemous) and on one's family (unless the whole family can come into faith with the individual).

- The person of Christ as Son of God, his death on the cross and consequent resurrection.

- The Christian theological books which raise doubts about the divinity of Jesus – Muslims around the world are taught that even Christians do not believe that Jesus was really God.

The most common ways for Muslims to become Christians:

- Through a vision or dream – usually either of Christ or of a person they have never met before, but whom they meet the next day and who tells them about the love of Jesus.

- Through healing – particularly miraculous healing through the prayer of a Christian after other sources of healing have been sought and have failed.

- Through the casting out of fear and/or of the evil spirit related to fear, by the prayers of a Christian. (Islam has no history of successfully casting evil spirits out of those who have become caught up in the occult.)

- Through reading a portion of the New Testament.

- Through friendship with a Christian, the quality of whose life is a testimony to the reality of Christ in daily living.

- Through reflecting on the inconsistency between the attitude of the Qur'an to Jesus (affirming his very important work as a prophet), and the practice of Muslims to hate Christians and to kill any Muslim who becomes a Christian. This causes some to investigate Christianity more thoroughly.

These points highlight the absolute dependence that one should have on prayer for the working of God in the life of a Muslim person.

The most common mistakes which Christians make when talking to Muslims

- Not being committed to Christian doctrine about who Jesus is and the fact that the Bible is God's revelation to us. Some think that there is room here to negotiate, but the Muslim is totally committed to an absolute understanding of who God is and to the belief that his complete and final revelation is contained in the Qur'an. When a Christian takes a weak position on such matters, this is seen as evidence that the Christian position is an interim belief which at best is pointing to where truth really lies, namely in the Qur'an.

- Not understanding the basics of the Christian faith and so not being able to explain the faith in clear terms and with assurance.

- Not being respectful towards the Bible, in regard to where it is kept in the house (for the Muslim it should be in a place of honour), or how it is referred to (it should be referred to with honour as God's written word). They see lack of respect for the Bible as evidence of the lack of holiness among Christians.

- Not recognising how much a Muslim already knows about God as revealed in the Old Testament. When a Muslim becomes a Christian, however, there is always an expression of great joy at having discovered that God is a personal God, one who relates to each of us such that we can actually call him, 'Father'.

What can you do?

Pray

As can be seen from the comments above, the most important first step is to pray. Look to God's Holy Spirit to lead you, giving you the right words at the right moment, and being at work in your friend's heart and mind.

Special events

Someone you are befriending may be willing to attend a wedding or a funeral of someone you both know, or maybe a special Christmas or Easter event. So make the most of these occasions.

Dialogue

See chapter six for a discussion of the meaning of this term.

The devout Muslim has much to teach us about commitment, obedience and the desire to see that God's instructions are carried through into everyday living. Christians have much to share about the saving grace of God in Christ and the assurance we have of being members of his family forever when in faith we accept his saving work.

Do not talk to a Muslim with the intention of seeing him or her converted; this will set up wrong attitudes and expectations. Rather, aim to share with them the Good News because Christ died for them and loves them.

Using the Bible

When the opportunity arises to refer to the Bible, remember that Muslims generally appreciate devotional material and that the Psalms are very acceptable to them. So this can be a helpful place to start. Over a period of time you could move from here to the Gospels as you increasingly share with them about Jesus. The Gospel of Luke is the preferred Gospel for a Muslim.

Muslims are keen to win you for Islam

Committed Muslims long to see the western world converted to Islam and many who live in a western country will actively promote

Islam. Anyone you talk to may be at the same time trying to convert you! Be ready for their arguments by knowing the Biblical texts that they use.

For instance, they will point out that Jesus said, 'Why do you call me good? No one is good except God alone.' (Mark 10:18 and Luke 18:19) In this interchange, Jesus is challenging the rich young ruler who has not identified Jesus with God, and so he is seeking to make him reflect on the implications of his own words.

Another text Muslims like to refer to is that Jesus calls himself, 'Son of Man' (Matthew 12:8 and see a concordance for other references). The phrase comes from Daniel 7:13 and this link means that Jesus used the phrase to refer to himself as the one and only person who was sent by God from heaven and would be coming again from heaven, but next time it would be in glory (the apocalyptic Son of Man). Jesus is the only person in the four Gospels who uses this term and it carries for him the inner meaning of the mission for which he came to earth, namely to bring salvation: 'The Son of man came to seek and to save the lost' (Luke 19:10).

Muslims counter the term 'Son', even if linked to 'of God' and the fact that Jesus often refers to God as his Father, on the grounds that we all are children of God (Matthew 5:9). What is important about the term 'Son' in the Bible is that it refers to the unique relationship which Jesus has with the Father. For further understanding of this relationship we need to study the rest of the Bible and not merely quote a phrase from it. The Triune God is not understood by Muslims. They think that we are referring to the Father, to Mary and to Jesus. It takes patience on both sides to explore the Scriptures to grasp Jesus' own understanding of himself. But a careful reading of the Gospels will lead the reader to this fact that Jesus did see himself and the Holy Spirit and the Father as *one*. See Matthew 28:19, Mark 1:9-11, John 10:30 and see Ephesians 4:4-6, I Corinthians 12:3-6, I Peter 1:2. Other texts you could refer to are: Luke 1:35; 3:22, John 1:1-4, 14-18; 3:16-17; 8:42-47; 10:31-39; 14:6; 20:31.

Muslims will also contend that when Jesus says the Father will send 'another Counsellor' (John 14:15; 15:26), the term really should be translated as 'prophet' and that Mohammad is this prophet. In response you could ask, if Mohammad 'proceeded from the Father' why did he die? Anything that is part of God must share his nature and therefore be eternal. Furthermore, what would be the point of yet another prophet when clearly Jesus saw himself as providing all the knowledge needed: 'I am the way and the truth and the life, no one comes to the Father except through me' (John 14:6)? The work of the Holy Spirit in leading us 'into all truth' is to help us to apply already revealed truth in every age and in every part of the world. Mohammad never pretended to be everywhere at all times. Only God could do this.

If you continue to hold a discussion on a friendly level then it is easy to say, in response to a question you have not thought about, that you would need to find the text and read it in its context and reflect on it and you would be glad to talk again next week.

1 In 614 AD Jerusalem was taken by the Persians and recaptured 17 years later by the Christian Emperor Heraclius. Ten years later, in 637, it was lost to the Muslims under Caliph Omar. The Muslims continued to control the Holy Land until 1099.
2 The Ottoman Empire started to disintegrate towards the end of the nineteenth century and came to an end with the loss by the Germans and the Turks of the First World War. The Holy Land came under British Protectorate from 1918 until the Zionist invasion of 1947.
3 Seyyed Hossein Nasr, 'The Islamic view of Christianity' in Hans Küng and Jürgen Moltmann, eds., *Christianity among World Religions*, Edinburgh: T & T Clark, 1986, pp. 3-12.

chapter 9

Hinduism

he Hindu[1] religion is very much more ancient than the Christian faith, dating from before the time when God gave Moses the commandments to declare to his people. While its beginnings are not really known, Hinduism goes back at least 4000 years. The holy writings of the Hindus are the Vedas (the name means 'knowledge') which are estimated to have been written between 2000 and 500 BC, and which include the Upanishads, and the Bhagavad Gita written between 500 and 200 BC. These scriptures are written in the ancient language of Sanskrit.

During its long history the Hindu religion has greatly influenced the culture of the peoples populating the Indian sub-continent. It may even be that a prior culture impacted the development of Hinduism; no doubt each shaped the other. Hinduism has no founder and no particular structure for carrying out religious practice. It is more a way of interpreting the universe, life and death than a creed. Hinduism is as much an expression of culture as it is of a particular view of life and death. It has no confession of faith, no identified divine revelation of truth as such, but the sages of old have shared their wisdom. While Hinduism does not promote a particular moral code, it promotes peace and declares that people can find it by controlling all desires and through turning their concentration on the divine.

The Hindu view of life and death is that when a person dies, it is only the body which is being shed. The soul will return to earth in a new body through the process of rebirth (reincarnation). Hindus believe that all human beings carry the consequences of previous lives in what is known as their *karma*. People's *karma* determines what suffering will befall them in their current life and whether they will return higher up or lower down the social/caste scale. (Someone who has been irreligious and done many bad things may well return in the form of an animal.)

This belief produces a view of life that can be called *determinism*. A deterministic view of life robs people of the desire to help those in need, or to be inventive in helping themselves or others in need. It produces a tendency to be arrogant in those who are born wealthy and in a high caste.

Ultimately, Hindus can only hope that as they accumulate good *karma* the soul will be saved from the endless cycle of rebirths and will become merged with the divine in the state of *nirvana*. This process will be helped by acts of devotion, by seeking to develop self control and by a search for purity. In these ways one prays for union of the self, the *atman*, with the eternal spirit, the *Brahman*. While regarded as the ultimate source of all being, the ultimate principle underlying existence, Brahman is not an active, personal being and so is not meditated upon or worshipped.

The three pathways (margas)

During the past 1500 to 2000 years, Hinduism developed three quite different paths for its expression.

Janan marga – the way of knowledge

This is the reflective dimension within Hinduism and it has generated six different philosophical systems. These are Nyaya, Vaiseshika, Sankya, Purvamimamsa, Vedanta and the more widely known Yoga. Behind these philosophies is the basic view that human life is temporary, but the soul is caught up in a cycle of death and rebirth until it finally can be released from this cycle and loses its identity by becoming bound up with Brahman. This state of Brahman is the bliss of a dreamless sleep. For the philosophically minded, meditation is the way to achieve this liberation from the otherwise eternal cycle of reincarnation.

Bhakti marga – the way of devotion

The philosophical dimension was seen to be too intellectual and beyond the understanding of the majority of the people. Hence, there is a devotional dimension in Hinduism known as the Bhakti movement. It sought to meet the instinctive longing in the human heart to know if there is a god and to find the best way to worship this divinity.

This gave rise to the development of the idea of deities. The chief of these deities was designated Brahma the creator, then under him was Vishnu the preserver and Shiva the destroyer. Vishnu and Shiva became the motifs for different sects to develop, each with their own incarnations of one of these two deities.

The devotional approach to these deities views the deities as personalities with whom mortals can relate. The deities however, have not called on mortals to relate to them, but it is hoped that they will listen to people's devotions.

Karma marga – the way of works

Those with limited education and members of the lower castes find the way of knowledge or of devotion beyond their grasp. These people usually have to work hard to survive and like to regard their work as a religious act. They hope that this together with worship (*puja*) to a local deity will eventually result in liberation from the imprisonment of their past lives. In the meantime they must accept suffering as their lot.

The belief in reincarnation leads to a great emphasis for the *Karma marga* on worship (*puja*). One must daily 'do *puja*', that is take flowers and food to the local manifestation of one or more of the Hindu gods. The faithfulness with which this is done will determine whether the gods will preserve one from natural calamities, bring fertility to the family and the land, determine the quality of one's next incarnation and ultimately cause one to break out of the cycle of rebirths.

For the *Bhakti margas*, the emphasis is on devotional exercises in holiness with the same hope of achieving *nirvana*. For the *Janan margas* there is effort in thinking and contemplation so as to achieve pure consciousness in which all reality is seen for what it is, namely, illusory. This concept of the illusory nature of everything around in known as *maya*.

A matter of identity

The identity of those Indians, Nepalis and Balinese who are Hindus is bound up with being Hindu and this identity gains practical expression in the caste system[2]. To cease being a Hindu means no longer being a member of the social caste into which one was born and thus no longer an Indian, a Nepali or a Balinese. Becoming a Christian is deemed by Hindus as being a public rejection of one's cultural and racial heritage and of one's family, and for a Balinese a rejection of the spirit of one's ancestors.[3]

The caste system no longer has the support of the Indian Government, but everyone knows their own caste and discriminates against those of lower castes.

The major caste groupings are:

- Brahmins (six per cent of the Indian Hindu population): the highest and purest of the castes. They are priests and landowners and in senior Government positions
- Other Upper Castes (14%): these are officially known as 'forward castes' and are usually landowners and merchants
- Lower Castes (52%): artisans and farmers will be found among these castes; they are economically and socially deprived
- Dalits (18%): the status of these people is so low that they are without a caste ranking; the Government reserves 15% of government jobs for these people; they are extremely poor.[4]

This question of identity is a major one for a Hindu, because the idea of reincarnation prevents a person from developing a clear perception of a personal identity. Hindus must therefore seek self-esteem from other sources and usually they find it in their community status, namely their caste.

For this reason, Hindus cannot believe that sensible people would want to give up the traditional religion and therefore their identity.

So they assume that conversions occur only among the lower castes who have nothing to lose, or because Christians are very aggressive and coerce people by bribes or lies.

Hindus believe that everyone has the divine in them so they see Christians as arrogant and offensive for ignoring the divine in Hindu people and declaring that they do not have the divine until they turn to Christ in repentance and faith.

Hindus believe that the divine is manifested in many ways, not only in the innumerable divinities (over thirty-three thousand named 'gods'),[5] but also in various natural objects such as an outcrop of a rock or a tree. They have no difficulty in accepting that there is a Holy Spirit and that Jesus is divine. What they dislike is the insistence of Christ's words that he is the only way, the only source of truth and the only one through whom a person can inherit life eternal with God (John 14:6).

How Hindus view Christians

Christians have been working in India since 1600 when the East India Company allowed chaplains to work there (the first known convert was a Bengali boy in 1614). Christianity first came to Nepal in 1737, but was banned thirty years later and did not reappear until 1952.

Today only three per cent of the Indian population declare themselves to be Christian. Although present throughout India, most of the Christians will be found in the semi-independent states of the north east, and in the coastal state of Kerala in the south west of India. It is estimated that most of the Christians belong to the lower social caste groups or the tribal people-groups of the north east and as such cannot relate to the upper castes.

Christianity is seen by Hindus as being a recent religion, even younger than Buddhism (which came out of Hinduism). For Hindus, the fact that Christianity emerged out of the Jewish religion means for the Hindu that Christianity belongs to the Mediterranean and European races. Thus they see Christianity as a colonial intrusion that has provided false hopes to those at the bottom of the socio-economic pyramid. Only the Orthodox Christians of Kerala enjoy an independent standing and status. This church claims to have been started by St Thomas the apostle and hence the church is known as the Mar Thoma Church.

Renaissance

Hindu beliefs were challenged by the appearance of Buddhism and again in the 13th century when Islamic forces invaded North India. One of the outcomes of this was the emergence of Sikhism (see chapter 10). Other minor regional sects also emerged and within Hinduism the *Bahkti marga* movement developed. Then in the 17th century the British established an economic presence and from 1856 until 1947 ruled a united India. As a result, the widespread use of the English language opened up possibilities for education for a much larger proportion of the population, even those of lower castes. Many among the increasingly educated population sought to grasp the thinking behind the religious practices. It was this which brought into being the *Janan marga* stream of Hinduism. Through this reflective group there have been new interpretations of the Upanishads and some new forms of Hinduism.

For example, in earlier centuries the view of the divine was that of an impersonal, unreachable power. Now the Hindu teachers were articulating the personal and moral qualities of the divine such as goodness, benevolence and love. This more recent personalised view of the divine opened up the possibility of actually worshipping God rather than 'doing *puja*' for the sake of some immediate or future benefit.

Raja Rammohan Roy (1772-83) was the first person to seek to reform Hinduism and to affirm that Christian ethical values were already contained in Hindu teachings. In his 'Society for the worshippers of God', he taught passages of the Hindu scriptures (the *Vedas* and the *Upanishads*) which emphasised the idea of one God behind all creation. Rammohan has been called the father of modern India.

Another example is that of the nineteenth century guru, Sri Rama Krishna (1836-86) who in one of his periods of meditation declared that he had a vision of Christ (others have also, such as Sadhu Sundar Singh who became a Christian and evangelist). This fact helped many to accept Christ, albeit as one of many significant divine beings. He discussed the possibility of liberation from the negative aspects of one's *karma* and therefore from suffering which is a result of sins in a former life. He was the first to emphasise that Hindu teaching was universally applicable and so opened the way to the idea of taking the religion to the West. He lived a devout life and developed the idea of a monastic approach and called these places for devotional living, *ashrams*.

The Christian missionary-teachers in India generated a questioning of the deterministic philosophy of *karma* and this caused one of Rama Krishna's followers, Vivekenanda (1863-1902) to form in 1897 the Ramakrishna Mission. This Mission emulated Christian projects such as the care of orphans, education and works of compassion. Here was a whole new approach to fellow humans. Because of the deterministic view of each person's state in life, there was in Hinduism no thought of caring for those in need and educating the lower castes. Now at least some Hindus were reforming their ideas because of the teaching of Christians in their midst.

Through his work and speeches, Vivekenanda fired a new enthusiasm for Hinduism in the young and impressionable generation of his day. He is well known for his address at the World Congress of Faiths held in Chicago in 1893. He used both monotheistic and polytheistic language. 'The divine' he said, 'is in all of us and we are in the divine. So we already have God in us and we should unleash this power.'

A growing number of people in the west today believe both in reincarnation and, as the New Age movement promotes it, the potential of humans to do whatever they desire: this is possible when one knows how to release this divine power within themselves. This thinking has come to the west from Hinduism and particularly from Vivekenanda and his disciples.

This modern approach to Hindu thought greatly influenced Mahatma Gandhi (1869-1948) with the result that he devoted his life to the upgrading of lower castes and the promotion of justice and peace. Gandhi maintained that his brand of Hinduism captured the best from Christianity, Buddhism and Islam. He maintained that passivity, even if it leads to suffering, is the preferable route for achieving social action. He had captured something of Christ's 'way of the cross'.

Although the traditional Hindu writings have no concept of a single ultimate personal divine being, the influence of Christians has been such that the Gita has come to be spoken of as a divine revelation and has sometimes even been called 'the word of god',[6] As a result much attention is being focussed these days on the Gita and new commentaries are still being produced.

Another modern guru is Sai Baba and his successor Sathya Sai Baba who believe that what they are promoting is a spiritual path for all to follow. He brings healing, to which a number of westerners have attested, and promotes a sense of peace and being relaxed in the sure knowledge that you are in touch with God in whatever form you like to know him.

These modern forms of the Hindu religion place a high value on peace, on supportive relationships, and increasingly on healing and on helping those in need. They accept Christianity as an alternative system for the same values, but are offended when Christians do not accept their religious belief as a valid route to *nirvana* (the ultimate resting place of the soul).

Cultural do's and don'ts

- As mentioned with Muslims in the previous chapter, be friendly and natural.

- Hindus do not eat beef. They respect the cow as being a holy representation of all creation.

- Hindus do not have congregational worship activities; their temples are places where a divine being dwells and festivals are held in the grounds. The Christian practice of gathering in a building to sing and pray to an unseen God is totally outside their experience.

- Because of the belief in reincarnation, Hindus view the body as having no further purpose or meaning and so prefer to cremate it.

- They measure spirituality by humility and acceptance of others. They are repelled by a door-to-door knocking approach to proselytism, but open to caring friendship.

Becoming a Christian

Stumbling blocks to becoming a Christian

- The importance of all members of a family, particularly those who follow the *Karma marga* tradition, to 'do *puja*'. This is to ensure that evil spirits are kept at bay and the spirit of the dead find their way successfully into the next reincarnation without bringing trouble on the family. One person failing to participate in these worship activities is seen to be very threatening to the whole family. For this reason, if a person insists on becoming a Christian the person is usually disinherited and thrown out of the home.

- Hinduism is an all inclusive religion. A Hindu is happy to add the name of Jesus to the plethora of deities to be worshipped. It is hard for a Hindu to accept that God has chosen to come into this world only in Christ Jesus and that the worship which God calls us to must be through Christ.

- Even though the caste system has been legally disbanded by the Government of India (as a result of Christian influence), it is so rooted in the Hindu culture that it is impossible to break away from it. Everyone is known by their caste standing. The Government has taken affirmative action to ensure that a certain proportion of the lowest caste people gain an education and are given government jobs, but they are often ostracised by the middle and higher castes.

Lower caste people are more ready to convert to Christianity because they have little to lose. Middle and higher caste people find that their sense of cultural identity is bound up with their caste and with being Hindu and that they therefore cannot become Christians without leaving their Indian or Nepali society altogether.

The most common ways for Hindus to become Christians

- A lower caste person being helped in some way by a Christian, such as through the casting out of an evil spirit or through compassionate help when in need.

- Through a vision or dream – usually either of Christ or of a place they should go to the next day – they meet a Christian who tells them about the love of Jesus.

- Hearing about the compelling, sacrificial love of Jesus which is offered as a free gift and which does not require a cycle of rebirths. Instead Christ offers us our identity forever. To put this in Hindu terms, 'Jesus took upon himself our *karma* so that we might inherit his *karma*.'

- Through understanding that true liberation of the soul can occur right now in this life in Christ ('If the Son sets you free you will be free indeed' – John 8:36) and that he is the truly personal God who has come to us and does desire that we respond to him in obedience. It is also reassuring to a Hindu to discover that God has made clear that we are 'destined to die once, and after that to face judgment' (Hebrews 9:27). For this to make sense to a Hindu, it needs to be made clear that humans are not merely souls camping in a body. We are whole persons created by God with a unique and unrepeatable identity. We are loved by God who has made it possible for us to be reconciled to him.

- Through reading a portion of the New Testament.

The most common mistakes Christians can make when talking to a Hindu

- Failing to recognise that Indians, Nepalis and Balinese people are very religious. There are different expressions of this and for some it is a thoroughly intellectual exercise. Failure to respect the careful thinking which some Hindus have done is offensive and arrogant.

- Not being clear about who Jesus is and that he is the way the Creator God has come into his own creation and made himself known to us. Failure to be clear about this results in confusion, since the Hindu already believes in numerous divine beings. Such confusion becomes a long term blockage to understanding the uniqueness of salvation in Christ and the reality of God as a personal God to whom we can relate through Christ.

- Requiring the setting aside of caste. Whilst caste is clearly against the biblical teaching on our oneness in Christ and on the love of God extended to all regardless of one's birth heritage, nevertheless it is not necessary to set aside one's caste-culture to become a Christian. It is up to the individual to look for the leading of the Holy Spirit. It is not our responsibility to transform a person.

- Failing to fold a budding or new Christian into a Christian community. Hindus who become Christian face the threat of being ostracised by one's own community. Therefore, it needs to be clear that the person is being converted into a new community, one that is caring and welcoming.

- Expecting (and saying) that food will be no longer an issue once a person becomes a Christian. Someone who has grown up being taught that it is a terrible thing to eat beef, cannot be expected to change, nor is there any need to change. The emotions, the taste buds and the stomach would all revolt at the idea of eating beef. We need to be careful not to press our culture on another person.

What can you do?

Pray

As already said in respect to Islam, the most important first step is to pray.

Find a point of contact

A conversation can begin with a discussion about the Brahman (see the reference at the beginning of this chapter); from there you can work your way to the knowledge we have of God as revealed in Christ. Or a conversation can start with the uniqueness of the holy man Christ, since Hindus understand about and respect holy men.

Another point of contact is the idea of salvation. God offers more than salvation from the cycle of rebirths, he offers a living relationship with him now and forever. Some Indian evangelists have found that the greatest impact occurs when the conversation starts with the offer of forgiveness of sins and the resulting rest in one's heart. This quickly leads to a discussion of the source of this forgiveness and peace through Christ.

Dialogue

As discussed in chapter six, this is a misunderstood word. It does not mean a half-hearted attempt to talk about the gospel but a conversation in which there is a genuine listening to one another.

The devout Hindu has much to teach us about commitment and devotion. Christians have the wonderful truth to share about the saving grace of God in Christ and the assurance of being members of his family forever for all those who in faith accept his saving work.

---

1. The word 'Hindu' was given by the Muslims when they invaded India around 1200 AD. It comes from the Persian for 'Indian'. Indians refer to their religion as that of the eternal teaching *(sanatana dharma)*.
2. In Hindi the word for caste is 'Varna Dharma' and is considered by some to have divine origins.
   The word 'Varna' means 'colour' and some scholars have shown that the idea emerged out of racial distinction between the Aryans (more European in appearance) and everyone else. But the most obvious basis was the determination of a caste by the work one did. So there are numerous castes and in many areas there are castes peculiar to the area reflecting the type of jobs pursued in that area. Sadly the caste identity then prevents the next generation from pursuing a job different to that inherited from one's parents.
3. The Balinese became Hindu during the period of Indian mercantile expansionism around 700 AD.
   At this time Hinduism also spread to parts of Indo-China, but this Hinduism was absorbed later by Buddhism. The Balinese absorbed Hinduism, but mixed it up with their traditional animistic religion. They see their unique Balinese identity intertwined with their type of Hinduism.
4. Statistical information taken from *Time*, April 13, 1992.
5. The most notable gods are Shiva, Shiva's son – Ganesha, Vishnu and Vishnu's incarnations, Krishna and Rama. There are also numerous goddesses.
6. See G. Parrinder, 'Is the Bhagavad Gita the Word of God?' in John Hick and Brian Hebblethwaite, eds., *Christianity and Other Religions*, Philadelphia: Fortress, 1980, pp. 111-125 (see p.119).

chapter 10

Sikhism

this is a relatively new religious movement which was started by Guru Nanak (1469-1539) in the Punjab (a large region in Pakistan and part of North India). It emerged out of a desire for a closer relationship with God than either Islam or Hinduism was providing. They believed that they could do this in a more formal and ritualistic way. Since the community came from one area they were of one clan and as they developed their own military power they became a distinct community.

Nanak drew his teaching both from Bhakti Hindu (with its emphasis on the devotional and the mystical) and Islamic Sufism (which also has a devotional element in its teaching). At the same time Nanak rejected much of the teaching of both religions. He taught that there is one divine being who is the true Guru and he is the Creator of the world. This divinity is usually referred to as *Sat Nam* (which means 'the true name'). Any one who sets his heart on finding *Sat Nam* can find him. *Sat Nam* is merciful, eternal and all powerful. This divinity is truth and has many manifestations. However, there is no suggestion that he is personal and there is no further description of him. One mystically comes close to him in the sense in which a husband and wife come close together as their love for each other grows.

Like Buddha, Nanak was against the caste system and the sacrificial rituals of Hinduism. Like Muslims, he was totally opposed to idolatry and to the idea of numerous divine beings (polytheism). His emphasis was on the mystical nature of religion in which there is only one divine being which is present everywhere (pantheism). Sikhism promotes a concept of salvation, which is drawn from Hinduism, namely liberation from the cycle of rebirths and a merging with the mystical universal soul, the Brahman.

Sikhism rejects the Islamic attitude towards women and promotes respect for them, although it does not view them as being completely equal with males.

Arjan, the fifth Guru leader, built the Golden Temple at Amritsar in north India and expressed antagonism towards Muslims and Hindus in a way that his predecessors had not. In 1606 Arjan was killed by the Muslims whilst in custody.

Sikhs have their own holy book, the *Guru Granth* (in Hindi, *Granth Sahib*) which means, 'the Lord's Book'. It contains material in six different languages, having been written by some 37 different teachers. Much of it is poetry in which *Sat Nam* is extolled and disciples are exhorted to holy living. The main part of the book is in the Punjabi language and this part is read out in the worship events.

The term, 'Sikh' means, a disciple. Traditionally, the five distinguishable characteristics of a Sikh male's dress are:

- no cutting of the beard or hair (and the wearing of a turban)
- a comb to keep the hair clean
- a metal bangle (to keep away evil spirits)
- black under shorts, and
- a dress dagger.

These five dress rules are known as the *khalsa* tradition and a male person who follows this tradition and who can read Punjabi (so as to be able to read the main part of the holy book) can ask for baptism (a simple ceremony of stirring sweetened water with a small dagger and then drinking the water). Women can also be baptised if they can read Punjabi and wear the bangle and black under shorts. A baptised person is expected to have a devotional life and to follow the rules of abstinence, namely not to drink intoxicants, not to smoke and not to eat beef.

Male Sikhs have as their name, Singh which means 'lion'. Women are known as Kaur, which means 'lioness'. Sikhs gather for prayer times, singing songs and reading the holy book in a temple (the Gurdwara). Chanting the songs is expected to bring one into union with *Sat Nam* and this should lead to a state of personal peace.

Cultural do's and don'ts

- Be friendly and natural as mentioned in previous chapters.
- Sikhs do not eat beef.
- Do not confuse Sikhs with Hindus. They do not believe in many divinities. They do not have idols. Their temples are places for singing songs and reading the holy book. Both men and women are equal and share in religious activity (although there is a male eldership to each temple community).
- As with Islam, show respect to their holy book and place your Bible in the home in a place of respect.

Becoming a Christian

Stumbling blocks to becoming a Christian

- Their strong family ties result in very strong emotional pull to stay within the inherited ethnic-religious system.
- The apparent immorality of westerners, all of whom are thought to be Christian. Sikhism has a clear moral code which is taught and the family has a range of sanctions to apply to those who break this strict code.

The most common ways for Sikhs to become Christians

- Through a vision or dream – usually of Christ.
- Hearing about the compelling, sacrificial love of Jesus which is offered as a free gift and which does not require a

cycle of rebirths. Instead Christ offers us our identity forever. With this is the wonderful knowledge that God is a personal God who cares about each one of us – 'O Lord, you have searched me and you know me…' (Psalm 139:1).

- Through reading a portion of the New Testament.

The most common mistakes which Christians make when talking to a Sikh

- Failing to recognise that Sikhs are very religious and that they have done some careful thinking about their faith.
- Failing to fold a budding or new Christian into a Christian community. Sikhs who take an interest in the gospel will be ostracised by their own community. Therefore, it needs to be clear that conversion includes entry into a new community, the 'body of Christ'.
- As with Hindus, care must be taken not to offend a Sikh's traditional diet.

What can you do?

Pray

As already said in the previous chapters, the most important first step is to pray.

Find a point of contact

Sikhs understand that ultimate salvation from rebirth is an act of *Sat Nam's* grace. Here is a bridge with the Christian understanding of God's grace. Another bridge is the Sikh's appreciation of suffering for the faith. Three of the earliest Gurus died for their faith. A discussion about this could provide a context for discussing the purpose of Christ's death. They see their holy book, the *Guru Granth* as divinely inspired and so appreciate our view of the Bible.

chapter 11

Buddhism

autama Buddha may have been born about 560 BC although some authorities suggest a much later date.[1] He was born in Nepal near the border of India. He was the son of an aristocratic Hindu chieftain of the warrior caste. He recognised the lack of spirituality and commitment in the Hinduism of his day and he sought by personal demonstration and teaching to bring about a revival. He also rejected the caste system of Hinduism and its sacrificial cults.

Much of basic Hindu philosophy became the base for Buddhist thought. For instance, the Hindu teaching on *karma* (that everything has a cause and these causes will be found in previous lives) and reincarnation is fundamental to Buddhist thought. However, caste distinction and the practice of spectacular mortification of the body during certain festivals were firmly rejected by Buddha. He taught that the caste system was a source of massive injustice and he described mortification as vain and useless.

Different traditions

Over the two and half thousand years of its existence, Buddhism has taken many different shapes. In each region it has been very much influenced by the local culture and prior religions and in its turn has modified the local culture. There are two major types of Buddhism; Theravada or Southern Buddhism and Mahayana or

Northern Buddhism. Theravada is followed in Thailand, Burma, Vietnam, Laos, Cambodia, and Sri Lanka. Mahayana is followed in China, Bhutan, Japan and Korea.

Theravada emphasises the simple life and takes a literal approach to Buddha's writings. Mahayana promotes a more liberal approach and tends to deify Buddha and his disciples. There are many variations within each of these. Some of these teach salvation to a blissful heaven and others salvation to a blissful nothingness.

True Buddhism has no belief in an eternal personal Creator God. Buddha was a great person, a great teacher and a great example to follow. He never declared himself to be divine, but he did sometimes designate himself in a way which invited reverence. For instance, this poem of his has been translated into English:

> I have no teacher anywhere,
> My equal nowhere can be found.
> In all the world with all its gods,
> No one to rival me exists.
> The Saintship verily I've gained,
> I am the teacher unsurpassed;
> I am the Buddha, sole, supreme;
> Lust's fire is quenched, *Nirvana* gained.[2]

In many countries Buddha is venerated in such a way that many regard him as if he were divine and prayers are offered to him with a view to gaining some material benefit or guidance. Many of his disciples are also viewed as divine, but as lesser beings than Buddha.

Some traditions within Buddhism believe that there is an idea of an impersonal divine being standing even beyond Buddha, this is the *dharma*. This idea is a reference to the foundational constitution of existence. Everything which exists and is righteous emanates out of *dharma*.

As one Buddhist monk has stated,

> The divine 'is not a person, but rather a force that is personified in the mind. The Awakened One shows us the way to happiness, peace and welfare by teaching us that no god makes man (*sic*) miserable or happy. The mind is where all evil and good come from. People create both misery and happiness for themselves...'[3]

Map 5: The presence of Buddhism in 700 AD

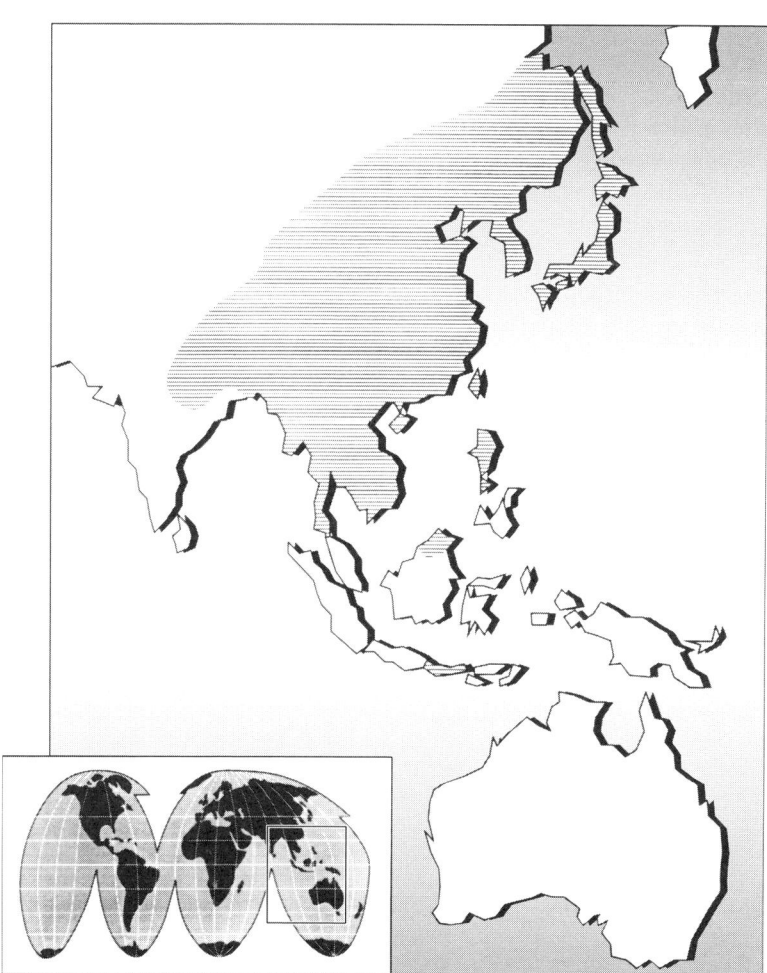

In its native Nepal and in India, Buddhism never took root. This is partly because the Hindu Brahmins could simply add Buddha to their pantheon of the already known divine beings, but also because of Buddha's rejection of the caste system. As it was only the higher caste people who were literate and able to read Buddha's writings, they had a vested interest in not allowing Buddha's teaching to become known.

Teaching

Buddha promoted a middle path between asceticism and self-indulgence. He established four 'Noble Truths', namely:

- suffering is universal,
- the cause of suffering is selfish desire,
- the cure for suffering is elimination of selfish desire, and
- the way to achieve the elimination of selfish desire is by the Middle Way, a technique which describes eight forms of discipline.

This Middle Way is referring to a middle path between the extremes of self-mortification and of self-indulgence. The eight steps (sometimes referred to as the Noble Eightfold Path) to be taken down this middle path are:

1. **Right views** – this includes the acceptance of the four noble truths and the rejection of unworthy attitudes and behaviour
2. **Right desires** – for healthy ends and rejecting cruelty and lust
3. **Right speech** – true and gentle
4. **Right conduct** – abstain from killing any form of life, from immorality, from stealing
5. **Right mode of living** – harming no one and being useful
6. **Right effort** – giving of oneself to maintain meritorious conditions

7. **Right awareness** – viewing the body as temporary and giving time to contemplation
8. **Right meditation** – concentrating the mind on only one thought and learning not to be distracted by thoughts to do with pleasure

Those who pursue these forms of discipline will achieve ultimate enlightenment, namely release from the chain of rebirths. This is the state of nothingness, *nirvana*, in which there is no further affirmation of self.[4]

For Mahanayas, *nirvana* is a place of rest and happiness in which there is no greed and no hatred. It is a state of optimum personal maturity and is considered to be the greatest goal that one can have. For this reason it can be said that Buddhism in its original form is not a religion, but a way to behave.

Since the emphasis is on how to behave, Buddhism does promote ethical behaviour, namely:

1. Kill no living thing (including insects)
2. Do not steal
3. Do not commit adultery
4. Tell no lies
5. Take no intoxicating drug or liquor.

Obedience to these precepts will improve one's *karma*. There are some extra rules for monks and nuns about living simply.

This emphasis on doing good overwhelms any teaching about truth. Buddha regarded doctrine like a diamond with many different facets, so he could teach seemingly opposing doctrines at different times. What he taught was relevant at the time for the transformation of the soul.

This inconsistency shows through in any discussion on the divine. Basically he rejected the existence of any deity. This view is upheld by the Dalai Lama on the grounds that 'a fiction cannot lead to any real and enlightening moral and spiritual progress.'[5]

Buddhists view Christianity as misleading, but nevertheless regard it as being of benefit in that it teaches love, sincerity, honesty and compassion. They consider that they have much to teach Christians about nature.

Cultural Do's And Don'ts

- Be friendly and natural.
- Buddhists do not eat beef and some will not eat any meat.
- They have a deep respect for nature and do not like to see trees cut down or animals, or even insects, killed.
- They respect their elders.
- Temples are places where one can undertake a personal act of devotion. They have no understanding of the Christian practice of congregational worship, but they are often interested in a special event. So it is acceptable to invite them to a special event such as a children's Christmas Eve service followed by supper in your home.

Becoming a Christian

Stumbling blocks to becoming a Christian

- The way Christians live is one of the major stumbling blocks. Buddhist teaching emphasises graciousness, treating creation with respect, not killing any living creature. Christians so often lack a gentle life-style such that Buddhists view Christians as brash, in a hurry and disrespectful of creation.
- Family links among Buddhists are usually very strong. A gracious spirit excludes confrontational communication. To become a Christian is seen to be a personal stand against one's own family – something too painful for many to try.
- Some Buddhists venerate Buddha and some of his disciples, but there is no teaching about the existence of the Divine Creator. In some Buddhist-influenced languages there is no

word for God, only 'the Lord' as an honorific title for Buddha. So the Christian revelation about the existence of one Creator God can be very hard for some to understand.

- Western thought forms and imagery are quite different to the Buddhist way of thinking and vocabulary. So much of what Christians say is just not understandable.

The most common ways for Buddhists to become Christians

- Through a sustained friendship in which the caring, self-sacrificing dimension of the Christian life is clearly evident.

- Through fear of an evil spirit which the monk can do nothing about and so the person turns to Christ through a friend, for release.

- Hearing about the compelling, sacrificial love of Jesus which is offered as a free gift and which does not require a cycle of rebirths. Instead Christ affirms our importance before himself and offers us our identity forever.

- Through reading a portion of the New Testament.

The most common mistakes Christians make when talking to a Buddhist

- Not being able to explain why we know that there is one God, who is God of the whole universe.

- Not being respectful about Buddhist teaching. The teaching may seem complex and hard to understand, nevertheless it is deeply thoughtful and strongly ethical. It occupies the mind of monks for a lifetime and provides a challenge to all to lead a worthy and pure life. Apart from monks, not many Buddhists have learnt about the teachings of Buddha, but they do know that it is a noble teaching and are proud of it.

- Traditional Buddhists will not eat any meat. As noted under this heading in the chapter on Hinduism, we need to be careful not to press our culture on another person.

- Not being respectful of the Buddhist culture – converted Buddhists have indicated that they are deeply grateful for all they learnt in their culture, although they are now thrilled to know that eternal salvation is available in Christ.

What can you do?

Pray

As already stated in previous chapters, the most important first step is to pray.

Find a point of contact

Friendship is usually an essential context for witnessing. As the very idea of God, of a living meaningful relationship with God in Christ, and of self sacrifice is totally outside Buddha's vocabulary, it is going to be the personal witness of you yourself which will be 'read' by a Buddhist. You can open up the opportunity to talk seriously about God by asking whether your friend understands Buddha to be a teacher, an example or the most significant source of truth. The person may know something about *dharma*, in which case there is a bridge here to talking about Jesus, the *dharma* who is personal and has made himself known.

Talk about Jesus

Buddhists usually have a deep respect for Buddha. They are capable of shifting that same respect to Christ. This will not happen easily. You need to talk about Jesus as your closest friend, as the One whom above all else, you respect and love because of what he has done for you. Allow your friend time to reflect on this and to ask questions.

Possible points of contact

The Buddhist teaching about suffering provides a useful point of contact. Christians and Buddhists agree that suffering is universal (Romans 8:22). The question of the cause of suffering can open up a significant discussion. We both agree that wrong behaviour such as selfishness is a major cause (see James 1:13-15, Romans 6:23) and hence the suffering of Christ is directly linked to the sin of all peoples. But the Christian believes that suffering will not be eliminated in a fallen world and we look forward to Christ's return when all suffering will end. In the meantime we can grow through suffering (Romans 5:3-5) and we are called on to help those who are suffering (Matthew 25:31-45, 2 Corinthians 1:4).

For many Buddhists there is a deep fear about evil spirits. You can indicate that God created us so that we could know him and he cares deeply for us and will keep evil spirits away from us if we ask him. This won't stop some illness or other difficulty, but these difficulties will not be caused by spirits but by other problems and God will stand with you and help you through these times of stress or difficulty.

A Buddhist's understanding of sin as such is limited. They know the five precepts listed above, but have no basis for understanding the fundamental nature of sin (namely to ignore God/to be god of one's own life) and that sin brings about selfishness, greed and pain in relationships. We know that we are born into sin and our desires have been twisted by sin (Romans 7:21-25). But through Christ's saving grace and the inner working of the Holy Spirit we are both forgiven and enabled to resist evil (Romans 3:21-27, Ephesians 2:8-10).

One way to help Buddhists understand about sin is to tell them that they never thank God the Creator for the sun and rain, the animals they enjoy and the food they eat, yet they pay for their electricity and gas and water and petrol etc. You can then ask is this not a sin? Then ask how to solve this problem. They will probably indicate, 'by doing good things.' You can share that Jesus can forgive (1 John 1:9).

Other contact points could be

- a person's desire to be released from the bondage of *karma* and the accumulation of previous lives;

- a person's search for an unselfish state of mind, or an attitude of deep devotion;

- a more satisfactory explanation of suffering and of death;

- a discussion about the after-life.

- the Sermon on the Mount provides a link in view of its practical promotion of an ascetic life-style.

- indicate your acceptance of the Noble Eightfold Path (with some modification of the fourth), while making it clear firstly, that we cannot follow these paths unless God is at work in our lives, and secondly that your eighth path would have to read, 'accepting God's forgiveness and presence in my life through Christ and his work on the cross'.

As opportunities do arise, do not expect to achieve much in any one conversation. Take time to listen by asking questions. Answer questions briefly, leaving an opening for the person to come back to you with a further question. Use the occasion of a well-known event, whether something in the news or one of the Christian (or other religious) festivals to get a conversation going.

---

1 This means that Buddha lived before Plato (428-348) and Socrates (470-399 BC) who were both in Athens.
2 Ollie M. Frazier, ed., *Readings in Eastern Religious Thought*, 2:174
3 This was written by Bhkku Chhin Channa of Wat Ounalom, Phnom Penh, Cambodia, May 3, 2000 in the *Cambodia Daily*.
4 *Nirvana* comes from the Sanskrit verb, *nirva*, which literally means, 'to extinguish'.
5 Paul J. Griffiths, *Christianity Through non-Christian Eyes*, Orbis Books, 1990, 162-170 and the XIVth Dalai Lama's quote is at p. 159.

chapter 12

Chinese religion and ancestor worship

'Chinese religion' is a convenient term for referring to the wide variety of traditional devotional practices of Chinese people around the world.

The religious attitudes underlying or emerging out of their devotional life are deeply influenced by Confucianism, Taoism, Buddhism and ancestor worship. There is no particular dogma taught other than those teachings which come via these religions. The practice of devotion also varies considerably, but the one practice which is fairly universal is the veneration of one's relations who have died.

Teaching drawn from Confucianism

Confucius was born in China around 550 BC (about the same time that Buddha was born). He worked for the government and became a widely acknowledged teacher. He drew his early material from ancient manuscripts which he edited and commented on. These were collected into four books and then he wrote his own work. The five books became known as the *Five Classics*.

From the ancient writings, Confucius promoted the idea that there is one Supreme Being, *Shang Ti*, and that he rules the world righteously and demands that all humanity functions as righteous people. This wonderful piece of general revelation promotes a commitment to a moral life ('to have a pure heart like a new born baby'), but it becomes rather confused by teaching about other mythological figures. For instance there is *T'ien* (sometimes translated as 'heaven') who exercises control over creation. But neither *Shang Ti* or *T'ien* created the universe – it simply exists. Another 'god' or mythical figure is *Shen*, a term used for special gods such as the god of fire, or the god of wood.

The range of gods are part of nature and so the order of human life should reflect the order of nature. Nature itself is constantly changing back and forth like the seasons of the year. This leads to the teaching that all behaviour should be evaluated on the basis of its usefulness. The impact of this teaching has been a pragmatic approach to life – what 'works' must be in tune with nature and so is good.

Human beings, according to the Confucian view, strive to imitate Heaven and their hearts must be aligned to Heaven's will. They do so however through their own strength and motivation.

Mancius, one of Confucians' followers took a further step to suggest that we are not only good in nature, but also naturally do good deeds. He taught that Heaven had created the world, loved its people, and wanted them to be prosperous and at peace. His famous saying states that there are four dimensions of the human heart – kindness (*ren*), righteousness (*yi*), politeness (*li*) and wisdom (*zhi*). The highest goal of life is to develop an inner sense of ethical commitment, deep empathy and compassion for others. Ethically educated persons should be honest, frugal and hard-working, trying to improve society and government.[1]

Confucius also expounded the ancient beliefs about the spirit world and that one's ancestors take their place in this nether world. Ancestor worship is referred to in the *Shu Ching* Book of History in which its teaching is dated back to 2255 BC. The acts of devotion are viewed as opportunities to be in personal touch with one's forbears and that by granting them due reverence they in their turn will watch over the living and ensure that they have a happy life. Devotion is also demonstrated through one's love and deep respect for one's elders, a respect that must also be shown by the young to those living and older than themselves. The supreme virtue is seen in a younger person showing an older person loyalty, humility and respect.

To the ancient Chinese mind, there was no greater sacrilege than not to worship or to pray for one's ancestors and Confucius sanctioned this belief, partly as a way of pushing the populace away from a general worship of spirits and the fear which surrounded that.

Confucius also taught ethical principles, such as the five virtues – righteousness, propriety, knowledge, charity and sincerity. He promoted justice, but had no idea about mercy or forgiveness. He believed that virtue was a matter of the will – a firm decision to follow after what is right, yet he had no concept of sin and broken relationships. People make mistakes or break laws and should be taught not to behave like this. Confucius' teaching provided the basis for training China's government employees until the formation of the Republic in 1912. At various periods he was venerated and temples were erected in his honour.

Teaching drawn from Taoism

Whilst Confucius drew on the wisdom of the past to outline right conduct in a world where human beings were central, Taoism (pronounced 'Daoism') emphasised the spirit world and its structure.

The possible founder of Taoism, Lao-tzu, may have been born around fifty years before Confucius. One tradition has it that they met each other and discussed their different views of the rightness of the ancient teachings.

He promoted the view that governments should not interfere with the daily business of the people and he taught ways of coping with the calamities of life. It is for this reason that the term *Taoism* emerged, being *The Way* in which one should order one's life. This 'way' is to conform to the flow of nature.

It is Taoism which introduced the concept of the *Yin and Yang*, used today in the New Age movement of the western world. The terms seek to explain the flow and ebb of life, the reality of matching opposites in nature (male and female) and in living (good and bad).

If one accepts the flow of life, then one ceases from being aggressive and lives as nature would have us live, without stress, without violence, perhaps without purpose, but in harmony with creation. This poetic balancing of opposites has been an inspiration for poets and painters in Chinese society.

This is the Taoist symbol which represents the continuous inter-penetrating light and dark and hence the balance between the good and the bad, the positive and the negative elements in every event of life. One can avoid misfortune by not disturbing this balance.

Unfortunately, this teaching tends to promote irresponsibility, indifference and passivity. Some see in this the reason for the slowness of the Chinese nation to develop the advanced ideas they had two thousand years ago. This teaching also fails to recognise the reality of evil and the possibility of there being a Supreme Being.

On the other hand, *Yin and Yang* includes the world of spirits and that there are good and bad spirits. This gave rise to the 'science' of *fung-shui*, the good and bad which controls nature and which must not be disturbed. Hence to maintain a good *fung-shui* an elaborate system of geometry is used to discern where and when action can be taken, in what direction the doors and windows of a building to be erected should face without disturbing the bad spirits.

The Yin-Yang motif and the Taoist philosophy of being in harmony with the universe and our own mind and spirit, has been taken up as a basic element in New Age teaching (see further in chapter 17).

Teaching drawn from Buddhism

For a fuller treatment of Buddhism, see the previous chapter. This religion came to China from India in the first century AD. It was seen at first to be 'barbaric' and so it had to change and adapt to Confucian and Taoist thinking to become acceptable (and is sometimes referred to as Ch'an Buddhism). For this reason it became impossible to separate the three main streams of religious thought and devotion.

Ch'an Buddhism emphasised the 'interior light', namely that such wisdom as we can access is already within, but in the final analysis nothing can be achieved because we are always distracted (perhaps this is an unrecognised awareness of sin). In the following two centuries, out of this Ch'an Buddhism emerged Zen Buddhism. This emphasised the belief that one must achieve by self effort. 'Look within, you are the Buddha' is a popular statement which has been picked up by the New Age movement.

Both Ch'an and Zen Buddhism teach that there is nothing greater than the individual: each person is a Supreme Being. Most people are not aware of their supreme status, but once they are, they will naturally care about the universe and love all living creatures in it. This is Robert Linssen's own statement in his book promoting Zen. He goes on to say:

> …the idea of considering religion and the rules which stem from it as an obligation is considered by the Enlightened Ones as a paradox…true religion (can come only) in the spontaneity of love and the most perfect liberty of the mind.'[2]

Chinese religion

Chinese religionists follow different combinations of the teachings referred to above and if they visit a temple will choose one they like which may have a more strongly Buddhist or Taoist flavour. Many pray only in their homes before photos of their parents and grandparents. They will have a family 'altar' and have a perpetual red light to keep away evil spirits. They are generally open to any religious teaching so long as it contains moral values and allows ancestor worship. This is important as their forbears are dependent on their prayers and the offering of food for their own happy life in the hereafter. Failure to provide this brings great offence and the ancestors may bring evil on their family through illness or disaster.

Cultural do's and don'ts

- Chinese people enjoy developing friendships and regard a meal as an ideal way to do this. They generally have no taboos about meat unless there has been a strong Buddhist influence in their lives. The easiest way forward is to work out your menu first and then check with your guests-to-be, as you would with a family which has some allergies.

- The Chinese respect their elders.
- Temples are places where individuals can undertake a personal act of devotion. They have no understanding of the Christian practice of congregational worship.

Becoming a Christian

Stumbling blocks to becoming a Christian

- The commitment to showing devotion to one's deceased elders which is deeply rooted in the culture-religion.
- The inconsistent way some Christians live, as outlined under this heading in the previous chapter, can be most unattractive to a devoted religionist. Chinese have a highly developed culture rooted in 2500 years of thought about how to live – the Path. Christians are expected to live out their beliefs and so to demonstrate in all they do the reality of a loving, reconciling God.
- The Christian belief in a Supreme Being who is outside and beyond all creation, yet able to enter into his own creation, sounds impossible to those who have never thought about the possibility of a God.
- As mentioned in the previous chapter, the western thought forms and imagery are quite different and much of what Christians say is just not understandable to them.

The most common ways for Chinese religionists to become Christians

- These are outlined in the previous chapter with the addition of a healing ministry. This is a typical way for Chinese in China to become Christians today. In western countries, Chinese are open to the moral teaching of the Christian faith and are attracted by the life-witness of Christians. This leads to questions about the Christian understanding of who God really is.

The most common mistakes Christians make when talking to Chinese

- Not being respectful about a person's ancestors, or not being respectful towards the elders in the family living with them.
- Not clearly defining the terms being used. Most of the words which Christians would use in a conversation about Christ have an equivalent in Chinese, but they have a different meaning. So Christians need to provide a definition for every unfamiliar term they use. Poor communication through lack of clear definition can cause long term blockages to understanding. Christians should provide Biblical texts as evidence for what they say, as Chinese generally respect an ancient writing.

What can you do?

Pray

Find a point of contact

Friendship is usually an essential context for witnessing. As ideas of God, of a living meaningful relationship with God in Christ and of self sacrifice is totally outside their vocabulary, it is personal witness that will be 'read' by them. The opportunity to talk seriously about God can be opened up by asking what your friend hopes to gain from the devotional exercises.

Talk about Jesus

As Confucius' teaching is at the base of the religionists' practice and as they respect Confucius, see if you can in discussion find some crossover points between his teaching and that of Jesus. They may not know much, but whatever they do know may well be similar to Christian ethics. You can then go on from the ethical point to talk about Jesus the author of creation, who is thus the One who not only knows how we should live, but who also changes our nature and our desires (John 16:5-16, Romans 8:1-16, Ephesians 2:1-10, Colossians 3:1-17).

Other possible points of contact

Discuss the appropriateness of honouring one's forbears. Highlight the advantages of continuity in family life, the benefits of mutual respect and the expression of caring love towards one another. Allow time for response and interaction. Look for an opportunity to move on in the discussion to explain how that real caring-love is demonstrated in what Jesus Christ did for all of us. Then carry on as the openings allow.

If your friend states that ancestor worship cannot possibly be set aside, then

- don't insist on a position early in the friendship/discussion,

- find out more about what your friend actually means by worship – is it just an expression of honour, is it an act of devotion, is it a prayer for the departed, or something else?

- be prepared at the right time to indicate an alternative, namely to pray giving thanks to God for the love of their relatives; and explain that before God this is a good way to honour them.

Remember that under the guidance of the Holy Spirit through the written word of God people can develop their own response to the gospel from within their cultural heritage.

---

1 As explained by Xiaoli Yang in an unpublished thesis, 1998.
2 Robert Linssen, *Zen – The Wisdom of the East – A New Way of Life*, Bay Books, 1972, p. 73.

chapter 13

Japanese religions

Ancient religions

From antiquity, every nation has had a tribal religion. This religion usually seeks to interpret the environment by attributing events, significant geographical features and certain animals or their movements to spirits. This primitive religion (sometimes referred to as 'folk') is generally referred to as Animism or Shamanism.

Shintoism

The primitive religion of Japan was probably Shamanism, as elements of this are still evident in current religious practices. It developed over one or two thousand years with its own stories of creation and of the appearance and significance of the Imperial family. In this more developed form, this primitive religion came to be known as Shintoism.

The importance of the sun goddess in the ancient religious folklore is reflected in the name of the country. These two characters mean *sun* and *source* or *origin*, hence 'place of the rising sun'.

The Shintoist story about the Imperial family is that they descended from the sun goddess and thus the Emperor was the source of Japanese life. Thus the Imperial family have expected to be worshipped. In 1877, the Emperor declared that the age-old religion of Shintoism would be the state religion and he outlawed Buddhism, even though it had been in Japan for some thirteen hundred years.

This ban lasted for only two years due to the objections of the people and so freedom of religion was granted until the Second World War. At the outbreak of the war, the Imperial Crown declared that Shintoism was not a religion, but a way of expressing loyalty to the Emperor. Everyone was to undertake the Shintoistic rituals as a public expression of honour and loyalty. All other religions were regulated during the war years. Many Christians were punished for refusing to undertake the rituals.

At the conclusion of the war the new Constitution allowed freedom of religion, but Shintoism with its emphasis on loyalty to the Emperor[1] has continued to be the official state 'religion'.

There is no authoritative set of beliefs and numerous Shinto sects have emerged, each teaching their own ideas about life. Some Shinto shrines are small and beautifully decorated buildings, others are like small roadside stalls in public places. In every shrine, it is believed that there is present a manifestation of the sacred, known as *kami*. These small shrines enable people to offer a prayer to the *kami* and gain some blessing from the *kami* by waving some incense-smoke over themselves as they walk by.

Confucianism

This came to Japan from China some two thousand years ago. Its appeal was its intellectual approach to reflecting on the spiritual and material environment. Those who follow Confucian thought would also be Shintoists and may also go to the Buddhist temple occasionally.

Buddhism

Buddhism came to Japan via Korea in the sixth century AD. It was mainly the Ch'an and Zen variety and it developed over a hundred of its own sects during the following centuries. It deeply influenced

Japanese architecture, generating the desire to give expression to the Taoist Yin-Yang and to the creating of an environment for peaceful contemplation.

Taoism

See description in previous chapter.

Modern Japanese religious movements

Since the 1930's numerous new religions have come into existence. Some are a development of the original folk religion. Others have taken into their thinking some aspects of one of the major religions. For instance, since the war a new form of Buddhism has emerged – the mystical *Nichiren Shoshu Buddhism*. Its origins have been traced back to a Japanese reformer, Nichiren, who lived in the thirteenth century.

This new religion developed in the post war period as an alternative to the bankrupt Shintoism (bankrupt because of the loss of the war) and is a major religion today. It requires very little of its followers. They have a ritual that involves kneeling before a black box containing the names of important people and rubbing together some rosary beads. It gives people something to belong to in a society that lost its self esteem with the loss of the war. It reinforces the work ethic which fundamentally in this form is an expression of materialistic greed (for example, followers have access to facilities like a private golf course, and an expensive lifestyle is promoted).

Other new religions are really secular clubs developed to meet the needs of the post war urban population. They are sometimes referred to as 'religions of personal advantage'. These groups are conscious of the deep unspoken hurts and needs of the people and seek to meet these needs. The hurts and needs have been identified by some as being the guilt complex surrounding the Japanese war, its atrocities and that it was lost. Others have pointed to the problems which emerge out of a very regimented society, robbing people of genuine choice and of an independent self-esteem (that is a self-esteem which is not dependent on the fact that one works for a particular company).

The size of the population (currently 122 million – half the size of the USA population, twice the UK population and nearly seven times the Australian population) in such a small group of islands (which would fit 11 times into the USA or Australia, but are nearly three times the size of the UK), together with the regimentation of school life and of public life, has robbed the Japanese people of their former sense of community. These new religions offer a well-developed context for community. They provide a wide range of services including a golf club, health facilities, holiday options and other facilities depending on their size. Many who belong (for a fee) to these 'religious' clubs would also occasionally undertake a ritual at a Shinto shrine or visit a Buddhist temple.

The Aum Shinrikyo doomsday cult, known for releasing sarin gas in Tokyo railway stations in 1995, may have emerged as an expression of frustration with the rigid Japanese society. It is interesting that its members have all gained good university degrees and are strongly bonded together. Whilst unlikely to meet a member of this cult in Australia, the criminal activities of this cult make it harder for Christians to witness to Japanese, as they tend to think of all religions beyond the traditional Japanese religions as cults which may have destructive intentions.

A secular mind-set

The religions of Japan provide a complex picture which few would understand. What Christians need to be aware of is that for a Japanese person, Christianity is just one of hundreds of religions, each of which meets some needs but none are of great significance.

The secular nature of Japanese 'religions' generates a secular outlook on life. A Japan survey found that generally there was strong resistance to pursue a religion since religion:

- weakens one's individuality
- blocks development of personality
- is there only so as to be able to call on the gods in times of trouble, or
- is a way to escape from the troubles of the real world.[2]

The fact that there is the one personal Creator God who deeply loves us and has entered into his own creation to take upon himself the penalty for our rebelliousness takes a long time to be communicated to the average Japanese person.

Cultural do's and don'ts

- Japanese respect their elders and particularly the Imperial family.

- They have no understanding of the Christian practice of congregational worship. Shrines and temples are places where one can undertake a personal act of devotion. To take a Japanese person to a Church service requires some explanation – it is usually better to take them to some other Christian event/gathering.

- They enjoy meals as a way of developing friendships.

Becoming a Christian

Stumbling blocks to becoming a Christian

- The inability to see that Christianity is any different from the plethora of other Japanese religions.

- Loyalty to the Emperor and commitment to showing devotion to one's deceased elders is deeply rooted and becoming a Christian may be perceived as withdrawing this loyalty.

- The Christian belief in a Supreme Being who is outside and beyond all creation yet able to enter into his creation, sounds impossible to those who have never thought about the possibility of a God.

- As mentioned in the previous chapter, western thought forms and imagery are quite different and much of what Christians say is just not understandable to Japanese people.

The most common ways for Japanese to become Christians

- Being befriended in a time of need or loneliness and discovering how genuine the Christian is and so asking about the Christ to whom the Christian is so loyal.
- A discussion about the purpose of creation and of life can open up a person's thinking and see that the Christian has an integrated understanding of the most important aspects of life.

The most common mistakes Christians make when talking to a Japanese

- Not being respectful about the Japanese Emperor or a person's ancestors.
- Not being clear about who Jesus is and what he has done for us. The idea that we have to do certain things to get ourselves right with God is not only incorrect but makes Christianity look like Japanese religions.

What can you do?

Pray

Find a point of contact

As discussed in the previous chapters.

Talk about Jesus

Your personal friendship with God in Christ will surprise a Japanese person, and yet this capacity to be in communion with the living Lord is what many would love to have.

Other possible points of contact

Discuss the appropriateness of honouring one's forbears (see discussion about this at the end of the previous chapter). Highlight the advantages of continuity in family life, the benefits of mutual respect and the expression of caring love towards one another. Allow time for response and interaction. Look for an opportunity to move on in the discussion to explain how real caring family love is demonstrated in what Jesus Christ did for all of us. Then continue as the openings allow.

1 The Emperor repudiated the legend of his divinity on January 1, 1946, although the rituals used for the inauguration of the current Emperor appears to have imputed divinity.
2 Fernando M. Basabe, *Japanese Religious Attitudes*, Orbis Books, Maryknoll, 1972.

chapter 14

The spirituality of Australian Aborigines

he original inhabitants of the great Australian continent have an ancestry which reaches back into antiquity. Forty thousand or more years is a long time to be on one continent with virtually no contact with the rest of the world.

Prior to the arrival of the white population, there were Aborigines living in every part of the continent. Professor Elkin's research has shown that two hundred years ago there were at least 300,000 Aborigines living across the continent in some 500 or more tribal groupings. Each tribe had its own language or dialect.[1]

An integrated view of life

The Aborigines developed an interpretation of their surroundings and their own place in it which gave value to themselves as people and meaning to their daily existence. To survive in what for the most part was a harsh environment, they had to be able to read the natural signs – of the weather, the movement of wild life, the presence of underground water and so on. This developed within them both a deep appreciation for their environment and a bonding to it, which is the envy of our modern environmentalists.

We have seen in an earlier chapter that Muslims believe the Shari'a law should be totally integrated with everyday life and with their identity. Similarly, Christians believe that the life which has Christ always at the centre is directed by the Holy Spirit and consciously surrounded by the presence of our Almighty Father. Such a life lived totally to the glory of God in the midst of his creation, will be transformed.

This totally integrated life can be described as 'spiritual' because of the recognition that we do not live our lives to ourselves, nor do we live only to share and participate in community. There is a living dimension beyond humanity that has entered this world and with which we are called to be in an eternal relationship.

As best as research to date has been able to show, the Aborigines of the past seem to have captured something of this truth in a remarkable way. Whatever aspects of the Aboriginal culture, belief system and ceremonies which could be identified as 'religious', were totally integrated with their identity as Aborigines. There was no distinction between secular and sacred, between ceremonies and cooking, between the stories handed down and religious beliefs.

Elkin has shown that to understand their systematised view of the world around them and their place in it, we need to pull together their beliefs about the spirit world, their totemism and their historical view of existence.[2] Much of this teaching is captured in stories or myths which are handed from generation to generation.

The 'dreamtime' motif

The stories, the totems and the presence of the spirit world are caught up in the idea of the *dreamtime*. With this came a variety of religious cults and secret rituals, about which only a small number of Aborigines living today know. For those who would like to know more about the religious practices of the past, the publications by Elkin and the Berndts referred to in the earlier footnote, can be readily accessed in most major Australian and university libraries in the English speaking world.

In relating to Aborigines today, we face a rather different cultural-religious context. The Aboriginal people today (known as *Koories* in many parts of eastern Australia and *Nyoongahs* in the west) suffer enormous loss stemming from the past. They have lost much of their tribal structure with its identified pattern of relationships, of elders and their unique way of making community decisions. Outside of the remote communities they have lost their language and ceremonies. Many significant topographical features with the associated land, have been taken away from them but in recent years some of these lands are being handed back to the tribal elders or community land councils. The major losses have resulted in a loss of identity, of self-esteem and of motivation to rise to the expectations of the Caucasian Australian community.[3]

Identity

It is this loss of identity which is so fundamental to understanding the attitudes and difficulties of Aboriginal communities today. Some communities continue to live on or near their traditional lands, but only after a century of displacement. At least some of those in remote communities (North Australia and Arnhem Land) have been able to preserve some of their traditional language and their understanding of kinship relationships which is foundational to their social life.[4]

Many Aborigines live today in urban centres or in country towns and have lost their tribal connections, language and identity. There is currently a new struggle to regain their dignity as Australian Aborigines with some looking to the reinstitution of ceremonies as a way of achieving this.

Christian Aborigines usually distance themselves from these ceremonies, but they do join with their sisters and brothers in the search for identity and dignity and they point to the repossession of some traditional lands as the one acceptable way in which dignity can be found.

Ceremonies are seen by most, though not all Christian Aborigines as a return to a belief in a world of spirits. It may be that some ceremonies have no reference to spirits and are really secular, that is, a cultural ceremony like a wedding breakfast. But many Aborigines hold strongly to the religious nature of their ceremonies and are opposed to Christianity as being inconsistent with their beliefs.

Those of us who are not Aboriginal need to understand that Christian Aborigines do not want to return to the old belief system.

It was an amazingly well developed and integrated approach to living, it did indeed establish a spiritual dimension and awareness, which at the time gave them an understanding of their place in creation, but there is so much more to be gained by being in a reconciled relationship with Jesus Christ.

It is worthwhile reviewing the religious past of Aborigines because, to the extent that a non-Christian Aborigine is aware of this heritage, there is here a wonderful bridge for communicating the gospel. Paul's letter to the Romans reminds us that people should be able to recognise the existence of a supreme being because of the wonders of the natural world around them and the capacity they have within them to determine areas of right and wrong. However, they lack the power of the Holy Spirit to do what they know they should and to turn away from what is unnatural and wrong.

It is also important that we understand the rich historical background of the Aborigines (and in other countries, of their original inhabitants) with a view to appreciating the roots of their identity and why that has been lost. This understanding can be a base for communicating access to a renewed identity in Christ: 'Everyone who is in Christ is a new creation' (2 Corinthians 5:17). This is not to say that the social-cultural inheritance is not important and valid. It is part of God's gift to us that we are capable of developing and handing down to each generation a distinct culture through our language, literature, art and ways of living in a community. We need to be deeply sympathetic to all who by reason of emigration from the people and land of their heritage have lost their social inheritance. In the case of the Australian Aborigines, we should encourage them to work out within their own community, and then within the wider Australian community, ways to re-establish some sense of their heritage.

Becoming a Christian

Most Aborigines have had some contact with Christians. Many will have parents who grew up on a mission station (as they used to be known). Those living in traditional communities will have had considerable contact with Christianity. Nevertheless, every generation needs to be introduced to the saving love of Christ.

Stumbling blocks to becoming a Christian

- In Exodus 6:1-9 we read that the Israelites 'did not listen because they had a broken spirit.' Likewise the Aborigines have a broken spirit and often find it difficult to listen. Patience and listening to an Aborigine's story can be a pathway to developing a friendship.

- The seeming irrelevance of the Christian faith, in view of the way that white people have treated them over two hundred years of European settlement in this country.

- The desire to recapture something of their traditional *dreamtime* and Christian's uncertainty of the links between this heritage and the knowledge of God.

The most common way Aborigines become Christians

- This is through the ministry of Christian Aborigines to other Aborigines. But Non-Aborigines can also share the gospel in the context of genuine friendship.

The most common mistakes Christians make when talking to Aborigines

- Talking too much and not listening patiently. It takes time to develop a relationship and this is best done through spending time sharing about the past, sharing personal stories and about listening to each others' ideas.

- Being in a hurry.

- Not recognising their spirituality.

- Generalising about Aboriginal life and belief – one needs to beware of stereotyping. Only in the context of patient friendship will a person's own ideas emerge.

What can you do?

Pray

Find a point of contact and develop a friendship

Talk about Jesus

Share your own stories of what Jesus has meant to you.

1. The first ever research on Aboriginal languages was undertaken by an Anglican missionary, L. Threlkeld who produced the first Grammar and Dictionary of an Aboriginal language and surveyed the languages across Australia. Since then it has continued to be missionaries who have taken an active part in preserving Aboriginal languages by committing them to writing and teaching the speakers how to read their own language. In the past sixty years there has been a growing interest among academic linguists and anthropologists. See Ronald M. Berndt and Catherine H. Berndt, *Aboriginal Man in Australia*, Sydney: Angus & Robertson, 1965. See also A. P. Elkin, *The Australian Aborigines*, Sydney: Angus & Robertson, revised edition 1974.
2. Elkin, Chapter IX, 220-261.
3. See for instance the Berndts, p. 216, for a description of how the use of art and ritual gave to each individual a strong sense of his/her own personal worth within the whole community.
4. Towards the end of the 19th century, Pastoral companies in Northern Territory and North Queensland had gangs out hunting down and shooting Aborigines on their massive pastoral land holdings. The coming of missionaries helped to stop this cruelty, together with the establishing of 'mission stations' which became safe areas to which Aborigines came to live. Many tribes were decimated during this period and so people were brought together who did not speak the same language. This resulted in the development of a *Kriol* language which has now spread through large areas of the northern part of Australia. See John Harris, *One Blood*, Albatross, 1990; and Henry Reynolds, *Dispossession: Black Australians and White Invaders*, Allen & Unwin, 1989, for more detail.

chapter 15

Baha'i, Zoroastrianism and Jainism

Baha'i

he Baha'i religion emerged out of Iran's Shi'ite Islam. It was started partly by Sayyid Ali Muhammad (1819-1850) who called himself the Bab (which in old Shi'ite thought referred to the 'gate' between believers and the unseen Imam). On 23rd May 1844 he answered questions put to him by a senior Mullah in such a way that greatly impressed those who heard him. He then wrote in a very short period of time a long commentary on the Quranic book (*surah*) of Joseph which has come to be considered a revelation from God.

This date and 'Scripture' writing mark the official beginning of the Baha'i religion. The Bab then wrote more works all of which are considered to be sacred. These writings include various laws and a prophecy that God will manifest a special person. This prophecy reflects the Bab's view of himself as the gate to the hidden Imam which in itself probably reflects Old Testament teaching about the Messiah.

Thirteen years after Sayyid's execution, Mirza Husayn Ali Nurf (1817-1892) declared himself to be the one 'whom God shall manifest' as promised by the Bab. He called himself Baha Allah ('glory of God'). He promoted the new religion and added to the Scriptures.

Baha Allah saw himself as the fulfilment of all earlier religions and the one whom God was using to make clear to all people throughout the world that there is only one God and that he calls all people to be united. They can find this unity in the truth revealed in the Baha'i sacred writings. These writings predict a 'Kingdom of God' in the sense that as people recognise the errors in their own religions by comparing with Baha'i scriptures and as they seek righteousness in accordance with these scriptures, they will bring about renewal, unity and peace here on earth. So the Baha'is seek to bring together all the major world religions for the purpose of worshipping God in a united form and for the promotion of peace.

Baha'is have suffered considerable persecution by the Muslims of Iran and in 1925 were declared by an Islamic court to be no longer a part of Islam.

The Baha'i religion, like Islam, forbids images, icons and idols. Worship consists of reading passages from their scriptures and sometimes from the holy books of other religions. In many ways it has become a secular religion, serving the goal of co-operation and peace rather than a genuine search for eternal life or the presence of the Divine in one's life here and now.

Baha'is tend to be very committed to their belief and resistant to any discussion which looks like identifying any one understanding of the person and will of God.

A discussion about Christ can be started quite easily as Baha'is accept that He was a prophet, but it is difficult to get much further. One needs to pray earnestly for the working of God the Holy Spirit in the mind and will of your Baha'i friend.

Parseeism or Zoroastrianism

Tradition has it that this religion was started by Zoroaster who was born sometime between the 10th and 7th centuries BC. This was the prevailing religion of the rulers of Babylon when the Jews were in exile there. It was the national religion of Persia until the Muslim invasion in the 7th century AD. Parsee means Persian and thus refers to the religion of the Persians. Over the centuries, Parsees migrated into parts of China and India and following the Muslim invasion, many more Parsees fled to India.

The beliefs include a commitment to one good creator god as described in their scriptures, known as *Avesta* (or sometimes as Ahura Mazda). There is also a force for evil (Angra Mainyu) which is equal in strength to the good force, Avesta, and which is destructive. There is a cosmic battle between good and evil and this is fought out in the lives of people on earth. Avesta calls on his creation to fight with him against evil.

Unlike Hinduism, they do not believe in reincarnation. It is said that believers at death come to 'the bridge of the separator' where they are judged by Mithra (an old god). If the bad deeds outweigh the good, then the soul goes to a place of temporary punishment. Those with more good deeds go to paradise. Good deeds include any action which limits evil or extends god's good creation. Everyone will be judged for their deeds, but hell and heaven are temporary places. Eventually, all creation will be reformed and heaven and earth will be joined together.

Worship of Avesta is impersonal. The 'fire' is regarded as the ideal manifestation of Avesta and so they have small 'fire temples' where one can go and worship god. The occult and superstition are a major element in this religion.

Because of the ancient inheritance of this religion, Zoroastrians are resistant to Christianity. One can only be born a Zoroastrian and so the population is rapidly declining. A discussion about Christ can develop in the context of their belief about what happens at the time of death.

Jainism

This was started in India by a Hindu, Vardhamana Mahavira (the Great Hero) in the sixth century BC. Like Buddhism it is an offshoot of Hinduism, but is no longer seen as part of Hinduism – it is a separate religion. Jainists reject the Hindu Vedas and have their own holy writings.

Whilst Jainism believes in rebirth and the law of *Karma* as in Hinduism, nevertheless, it strongly asserts the individual identity of the soul and therefore the worth of each individual. Mahavira spoke strongly against the Hindu idea of caste, against the plethora of divine beings and against the slaughter of sacrificial animals.

They focus their worship on the 24 Saints (*Jinas*). The purpose of this worship is to contemplate the holy behaviour of the Saints and to reflect on how to follow their example. There is eternity, but only in the sense that everything is eternal. This doctrine has brought about a situation in which there is no concept of a Divine being, Jainism emphasises the importance of the individual living a holy life, which means

- not to hurt any living being, animal or insect,
- to abstain from violence, and
- to be righteous through humility, purity, truthfulness, restraint, austerity, voluntary poverty and spiritual obedience.

The monks add to this some 22 'trials' including fasting as ways along a spiritual path which will result in getting rid of some past bad *karma* and so enable one to move nearer towards *nirvana* in future rebirths.

This is an ascetic and legalistic religion. Its emphasis on not hurting any living being means that they are unable to pursue agriculture or animal husbandry. Over the centuries they have concentrated on commerce and are today expert business people.

What has been said about the Hindus' view of Christianity generally applies to Jainists, except for the added fact that they view themselves as already practising a reformed Hinduism and so are not in need of any further reform.

chapter 16

Migrants with a Christian heritage

not all migrants to western countries come with an Islamic, Hindu, Buddhist or other religious background; some come from families which have traditionally been Christian. Not only the European migrants, but also some from Asian, Middle Eastern and African countries will tell you proudly of their Christian heritage.

2000 year old churches

It is a challenging fact that Christ came to a Middle Eastern country and the gospel was first proclaimed in Jerusalem and Samaria. It was then taken to Damascus (which is still today the capital of Syria). St Paul went further afield and took the gospel to the region of Galatia which today forms part of Turkey. Tradition has it that St Mark took the gospel to Egypt and St Thomas to India. Although today the majority religion in Syria, Turkey and Egypt is Islam and India has remained Hindu (except in the State of Kerala where Thomas went), nevertheless there is still a Christian community in these countries.

Continuity of these historical churches

Within the first few centuries of the Christian era the gospel was taken to all the countries around the Mediterranean Sea. This occurred regardless of the persecution of Christians which persisted until Constantine the Great was converted in AD 313. During the following three centuries the Christian Church became well established in these countries.

In the seventh century, persecution of Christians started again as a result of the Muslim invasion of all the countries of North Africa and the Middle East. Notwithstanding this persecution, the Christian church continued to exist even though it shrank in size. These historical churches have survived various waves of persecution and maintained their witness to the Cross through their suffering.

Proselytism

Most of these historical churches (Orthodox and Catholic) consider that everyone born into a family that regards itself as Christian is a member of the Church to which that family has traditionally belonged. This view has helped to preserve the church in the midst of antagonistic environments, thus not allowing Muslims to claim that a person has no religious connection at birth and therefore has to make a decision at the age of discernment. Both Muslims and Christians link children to their parents' religious heritage.

Some migrants with Christian grandparents have never attended their family's traditional church and will admit that their own understanding of their Christian background is minimal. They will indicate, just like many westerners, that they were baptised as babies and have had their marriage blessed in the church, but they never go to church and have no understanding of the gospel.

Many first generation migrants are faithful church attenders but some, to their great disappointment, find that their children have been caught up with the secular mindset of their new home country. Those of the second and following generations usually have little or no desire to attend the church of their parents and they know little of the love of Christ.

When such people discover the love of Christ and respond in faith to Christ's free gift of salvation, they need to determine which congregation will be their spiritual home. If the decision is to attend a congregation other than the one of their parents, there is sometimes an expression of deep concern by the parents and/or by the leadership of the traditional family church. The act of encouraging a person to change denominations is known as proselytism. The word 'proselytism' was originally used of Gentiles who adopted the Hebrew faith. In the second century AD it was used by those who converted to Christianity. Today it is used when people are attracted away from the church in which they were baptised to another denomination. Sometime the phrase 'sheep-stealing' is used to mean the same thing.

In a democratic society and particularly in our western society where individualism is a supreme value, one can only protest that everyone has the right to worship in whatever congregation she or he chooses. Those who have rarely been to church may not feel any commitment to the denomination of their parents. Furthermore, if the Sunday service is conducted in an ethnic language that the children do not speak, then it is likely that they won't feel comfortable.

On the other hand, we need to remember that first generation migrants have generally brought with them a strong sense of community and of the solidarity of the extended family. So they will quite naturally be upset when one member of the family moves off in a different direction. These are cultural attitudes and they can touch feelings very deeply; love, care and wisdom are required.

Choosing a congregation

Clearly, there is no congregation that conducts its affairs in a way that could be considered perfectly biblical. In fact, the Scriptures do not lay down a complete set of rules about the life of the church, although they do provide some guidelines, many examples and ideal standards. While contact with other congregations can help us to see the faults in our own congregation, seeing these faults would not normally cause us to move out to another church.

In considering on what basis a decision about church membership could be made, the following essentials should be taken into account:

- Is God, Father, Son and Holy Spirit at the centre of the worship life of the congregation? (Hebrews 2:9 'But we see Jesus…crowned with glory and honour…by the grace of God'.)

- Is the word of God clearly taught so that those present are being discipled? (Matthew 28:19 'Go therefore and make disciples…')

- Is there freedom to study God's word for oneself and with others? (1 Thessalonians 1:8, 2:13 'the word of the Lord echoed out from you…you received the word of God which is at work in you.')

- Is there a spirit of worship and of supportive fellowship that enables one to feel that this congregation would be a spiritual home?

Other issues to consider are:

- Sometimes division can be created in a family if the parents or older siblings see themselves as members of their traditional church, and a member of the family who has a new enthusiasm for the gospel starts to attend a different church. Such a division can bring antagonism and may be damaging to the gospel.

- The minister of the church to which the family belongs may have given considerable time to helping the family and/or the one who has a new faith. Rejection of that church can be taken personally by the minister and may arouse a deep sense of frustration.

Any decision to change from one Christian tradition to another should be made after prayerfully considering the above guidelines; even then it may be preferable to make one decision for the time being with a view to a different decision in the future. It is often wisest to make a tentative decision, to act on this, but to continue to reflect on the issues surrounding the decision for some weeks or even months before making a firm and final decision.

Great wisdom is required on the part of anyone counselling a person who has rediscovered, or discovered for the first time, the joy of a lively faith in Jesus Christ. If such a person is living with a family who attend the church linked to their ethnic roots, then it may be wisest for the person to continue to attend the congregation with the family. Such congregations usually conduct services in the mornings. This would leave the person free to attend a different congregation in the evening where the language, the teaching and the fellowship is more relevant to that person's present circumstances.

If your friend decides to worship in a congregation different to your own, affirm your friend in this independent decision. Ask if you can continue to meet for Bible study and remember that it is not you, but the Holy Spirit who has brought your friend to faith in Christ and who will continue to be at work, convicting, guiding and sanctifying.

Appreciating other Christian communities

Most of us participate in our own Christian community and have little to do with members of very different communities. This means that we are comfortable with the way our congregation worships and is administered. But when we spend time with a different congregation, we find ourselves comparing and contrasting the liturgy, the fellowship, the way teaching is provided and the way leadership is exercised. We may recognise weaknesses in our congregational life and/or we may be critical of numerous aspects of the 'foreign' congregation.

If you do have contact with a person who traditionally belongs to one of the historical churches, then it could be instructive to go with your friend to a church service. It is preferable to do this with someone who understands the service and can interpret the liturgy (both as to what is happening as well as some translation). Ideally you should spend some time with such a person after the service to reflect further on the meaning of its various parts. This would demonstrate to your friend a genuine interest in his or her liturgical heritage and cultural roots.

It is easy to be critical of churches very different from your own; but we should have in mind that God in his sovereignty has been at work through a variety of churches down the centuries. For instance, the Orthodox churches can look back to the early centuries when the leaders of their churches were deeply involved in theological debate, and we have benefited from these debates and the conclusions reached. We should also remember that many of the

Orthodox churches have sustained a Christian witness in the midst of great opposition by either Islamic or Communist governments. At the same time these churches may need some reformation and we can only pray that this will come.

Other ethnic churches do not have a long tradition and would be described as Protestant churches. The only difficulty could be if the church is using a language which those born in Australia can barely understand. On the other hand, some of these ethnic churches provide an opportunity for people of similar background to have fellowship and to provide a context which would be acceptable to a non- Christian friend of the same ethnic background.

chapter 17

The New Age Movement

A non-religion of westerners

he term, *New Age Movement* refers to a wide range of spiritual substitutes current in western society which promote the idea that humans have unlimited potential to achieve whatever they would like to achieve. In particular, there is the potential to transform our earth planet into a 'new age' of balanced ecology, harmonious relationships and personal success (referred to as the age of Aquarius). The term was promoted by Annie Besant who was a leader of the Theosophical Society (a religious movement which emerged out of Hinduism).

The New Age movement is fundamentally a turning away from Christianity to pre-Christian pagan beliefs or Eastern religious ideas as a source of spiritual satisfaction or as a source of power over one's environment. The New Age is not an organised religion. The term is used to refer to a large number of different and often overlapping beliefs about creation, the self, the world of spirits and of unseen powers. These beliefs are being promoted in the western world, but many of the ideas have their roots in Hinduism and/or Buddhism and/or the occult. So those who follow some New Age idea are generally doing so as a way of rejecting Christianity as they understand it or because they have met some really supportive friends who have shared with them their New Age concepts. Naisbett in his *Megatrends* estimates that ten per cent of the western population follow New Age beliefs and that USA corporations spend $4 billion annually on New Age consultants to boost the productivity of managers and sales staff.[1]

The range of New Age attitudes generally can be summed up as follows:

Eastern spirituality/mysticism

The 1960's and early 1970's were times of great frustration among young people in western society. Disillusioned about the post-war goals for economic development and angry about being forced to participate in the Vietnamese war, they sought to explore ways to escape mentally and emotionally the stupidities of humans tearing each other apart and to discover new ways of thinking about the world and themselves. Beatnik music, protest songs and for some psychedelic drugs were means whereby they could change their state of consciousness.

This new consciousness included a rejection of goal-oriented existence and Christianity. It also included a search for a simple lifestyle and strong friendships among the like-minded. This period was referred to as the *psychedelic era* or the *new consciousness movement*.

As this generation grew into adulthood, many explored other routes to achieve the same ideals. One of the leaders in this movement was the pop group, the Beatles. In the mid-1960's they spent time at the Maharishi Mahesh Yogi's Ashram in India where they learnt about Transcendental Meditation and its offer of a higher state of consciousness. This state is supposed to be achieved by concentrating on a 'mantra', that is a secret word, until one's thoughts reach beyond normal human reason to a super-conscious state. This is a state of enlightenment which cannot be put in words. It is described by those who believe they have achieved it as a mystical experience in which one feels at one with the universe, free from the restrictions of language, culture and emotions, doctrine and expectations.

The Beatles promoted the transcendental meditation view of a higher state of consciousness through their songs. Since then, the promotion of various approaches to meditating on mantras has been undertaken by followers of Zen Buddhism, Yoga, Hari Krishna, Sai Baba and the Divine Light Mission, among others.

The Hindu and Buddhist belief in reincarnation

This is the belief that the human soul never 'dies' but is reborn in another body when physical death occurs. With this teaching comes the idea that the soul does carry with it a permanent record of all of a person's good and bad deeds, what the Hindus call *karma*.

Astrology

Those who study astrology believe that the stars and the configuration of the planets determine a person's successes and failures in life. Astrologers draw a great deal of information from ancient pagan beliefs and current scientific knowledge in the field of astronomy. With this information they seek to link a person's birth and other significant events with the movement of the planets. They maintain that this knowledge enables a people to better understand their personalities, to see how past events fit into an overall direction in their lives and to predict some future events.

The Occult

This is the practice of making contact with unseen powers. There are many different ways to do this. Some say they have psychic powers that enable them to discern the future or the past – particularly 'previous lives'. With this comes the view that a great psychic force or a 'god-like' force is evident in some piece of crystal or basalt rock, or a shape like a pyramid, or even in all creation.

Then there are the ancient pagan practices of contact with evil spirits through white or black witchcraft, satanism, ouija boards, channelling and similar activities. This has led to the belief that people can find within themselves the most valuable source of physical and spiritual energy; and that they can, through appropriate concentration and understanding, do whatever they want to do.

This is a new form of humanism (the idea that there is nothing beyond this life and that humans can and should look only to themselves to improve their existence). It clearly eliminates all responsibility to a creator God and it promotes the self as being part of the divine and having the capacity to access divine power.

Nature or Folk Religions

This is a revival of primitive religious ideas pursued by the American Indians and the English Druids in a pre-Christian era. Followers seek to learn all they can about these pagan religious activities and then practise them.

Ecology

Not all who promote care of the environment are New Agers but some who have been deeply involved in ecology find themselves sharing with those who have made ecology into a kind of religion. The intense desire to fight for the preservation of wild life, forests and so on takes some people beyond scientific facts to a search for a deeper and perhaps more emotional argument. Such an argument promotes the belief that all creation is divine (Pantheism). This was a Hindu concept that became more strongly articulated in Buddhism.

Many of those who have become pantheistic in their thinking take a strong stand against eating meat and have sought to popularise the age old beliefs in herbal medicines (homeopathy) and/or promoted a new understanding about health food.

Human potential movement

Some who have been attracted to eastern spirituality/mysticism and/or the Hindu belief that we participate in the unseen divine force that permeates creation, have concluded that within the self is the source of energy needed to bring about personal transformation. This has led some in the world of business management to search for a new framework of thought within which they can understand themselves and pursue their goals of success. These are achievement-oriented people who maintain that you are what you want to be.

Out of this stream of thought has emerged the 'human potential movement'. The Gurus of this movement offer (to those who can afford to pay for it) a way of becoming a 'spiritual illuminati' – a people who have higher wisdom than everyone else and so can be described as having a new enlightenment. The claim is that this special understanding (gnosticism) or super consciousness gives rise to a capacity to become whatever you want to be, to achieve whatever goals you set for yourself and to control your destiny.

Becoming a Christian

Why people turn to the New Age

People find themselves thinking about the ideas in one or more of the categories above as a result of being disillusioned about what is going on in the world and a longing for one or more of these goals:

- To gain *peace* within themselves in the midst of a fast moving and confusing world;

- To gain *power* over their own destiny including the ability to overcome some major difficulty or stress;

- To tap the full *potential* and so be healthy and/or successful;

- To achieve *prosperity* and so maximise enjoyment of life; and/or

- To gain a fresh *perception* of the universe (a new world view) in which all creation is seen to be divine.

People may find it intriguing to explore new ideas or they may have an earnest desire to go beyond the known world and make contact with untapped powers either within or beyond themselves.

Generally, they are drawn into New Age solutions through a friendship, a business contact or a management seminar. This is the intellectual route. Others, however, come into the New Age movement through the occult or other forms of mysticism; these are not intellectual, but emotional routes. These people have unsatisfied longings that sometimes cannot be expressed in words, e.g. the feeling of not being at peace with themselves or of having unmet emotional needs, or a fear of the unknown and a desire to explore it. Often they find some satisfaction for their own imaginary longings by creating their own imaginary world (via occult practices or mystical reflection).

Each New Ager you meet will probably be investing energies into a different 'world', a different ideology from every other New Ager. So it is not possible to predict the ideals and hopes of any one person. You need to inquire and then relate to what is told to you.

The Basic Problem

Notwithstanding the diversity of motives mentioned above, one thing that tends to dominate all streams within the New Age movement is the fundamental concept contained in the daily Hindu greeting: *Namaste*, which means 'I (or the divine in me) bow down before the divine in you'.

As Shirley MacLaine, the high profile New Age guru claims, everyone is God. If everyone is God, then no *one* is God, i.e. there is no Divine personal creator to whom creation owes its existence and allegiance. This allows everyone to consider that they are responsible solely to themselves.

Such a position has these consequences:

- There is no right or wrong for all people – everyone determines his or her own moral codes;
- No one really matters other than oneself. Since the source of one's integrity and the goal for one's life are entirely dependent on self, then one must place *self* at the very centre of all decisions and motivations;
- All individuals are responsible for personal salvation from earthly woes; and
- The search for the Divine within produces an intensely selfish, inward looking person.

Clearly the ultimate deception of the New Age movement is that the self is God. It requires a massive shift in thinking to turn away from self and look outwards to a transcendent God who saves and transforms us, frees us from ourselves and brings us eternal peace and eternal membership of his family.

What can you do?

There are three major differences between New Age people and those who follow other religions.

- New Agers are westerners – this is not a religion of Africa, Asia or the Middle East.

- New Agers are not devout followers of an historical religion. They have no God to worship, no prophet to follow and no set of ideals to obey.

  According to the thinking/reflection framework that New Age people generally have developed for themselves, any and every exploration within oneself is legitimate, so long as it affirms the importance of self; and all religions/mystical or unexplainable experiences are valid for the individual.

  As a result nothing that has been said in the previous chapters on other religions, even in respect to Hindus and Buddhists, is likely to be of any help to you in your efforts to build a communication bridge.

  Furthermore, these people have grown up in a community where Christianity, albeit nominal, is the dominant religion. They think they know what Christianity is all about and they have already determined to reject it. This makes it very difficult to develop a context in which a New Ager would be willing to dialogue with you.

- Finally, some New Agers are caught up with the occult and so any real discussion with them could develop into a spiritual showdown. Generally we would be wise not to tackle such a power-encounter on our own. Christ's presence is promised when two or three of his people gather together and ask for his guidance and the power of the Holy Spirit. For these reasons the following steps are suggested.

Prepare for spiritual warfare

Ask your church bible study group to pray with you about when and how to reach a person you know who is involved in some aspect of the New Age movement. Reflect together on the meaning of Paul's teaching in Ephesians 6:10-18. Ask yourself whether you are equipped with God's protective armour. Ask the group for their wisdom, guidance and support.

Demonstrate your faith in your life

The witness of our lives will have the most influence in achieving grounds for communication. New Age people believe in themselves, in their inherent capacity to achieve whatever they want to achieve. They consider a belief in God to be a dependent relationship in which people lose both self-esteem and freedom to be whatever they want.

Generally, New Age people do not consider that truth can be captured or described in words or even that there *is* objective truth. Their mind-set is influenced by mysticism and/or experience. Whatever a person has experienced and believes, is truth for that person. Thus they need to see in you as an individual, and ideally in the life of your local congregation, a demonstration of the peace and of the spirit of caring for others and for creation that they themselves are looking for.

There should be a consistency between ideas and behaviour, between truth as we proclaim it and obedience to this truth, not only in *what* we do, but also in the *way* we do it. Our faith is not only a cerebral commitment. Others need to see an emotional commitment whereby real serving love bubbles through as we talk to others.

Develop friendship dialogue

As intellectual argument on its own rarely wins anyone for Christ; it is best to start with friendship. Have lunch in the lunchroom at work or on the lawn at college, or offer assistance to a neighbour. Listen to your friend's conversation and ask about his or her hopes and goals. Follow through their response by asking which hopes/goals have not been achieved.

Then probe a little deeper and discuss one of your friend's hopes (e.g. a desire for long term friendship, a concern about the next life or an aspect of his or her immediate life).

Seek then to share your own experiences of God at work in your own life and the fulfilled hope of being accepted by God as a member of his kingdom forever. Then as opportunity allows outline the assurance you have of God's Holy Spirit at work in you, for instance in:

- *Applying* God's saving work to you personally every moment of your life;

- *Guiding* you in the study of his written words so that you are able to grasp God's truths which are the highest truths of all;

- *Enabling* you to resist doing things or concentrating on ideas which are not in character with God, the Creator of the whole universe;

- *Keeping* you so close to the unseen God that you can genuinely call him Father and know that to him you are more important than all creation (because he took upon himself the punishment due to you for ignoring him and therefore trying to be God of your own life).

Be prepared for a doctrinal approach

When a level of trust or respect has been developed between you and your friend, prayerfully look for the opportunity to stress the difference between:

- Searching for peace or trying to make meaningful contact with the divine in one's self; and

- Accepting what God has already done and offers us, namely to be part of the one and only Divine family. God is not an impersonal force, but a real person who calls us to be in a real and eternal relationship with him.

We may be able to point out that the problems in society are not because people are ignorant of their divine potential, but because they have rebelled against a personal and moral God.

As the discussion moves on, aim to challenge the person with the liberating fact that we can become 'new people' in Christ (2 Corinthians 5:17).

Have a caring approach

Many people move into New Age thinking because they seek answers to personal problems – the failure of orthodox medicine to cure a continuing ailment; stress; bereavement; or because they long for an experience which will excite them in the midst of an otherwise boring existence.

Christians are concerned for the whole of God's creation and in particular for people. We are called both to proclaim the Gospel and to meet the physical needs of those in great difficulties (Matthew 25:31-46). As congregations and/or as individuals we can show our concern for those in need and for important social issues, and through this demonstrate that God is Lord of all and that he has promised a new creation. In the context of such a global concern, we can give expression to God's saving work and his call to all to turn to him in repentance and faith.

---

1 Warner Books, New York, 1982, pp. 259, 273

chapter 18

Community challenges
When other religious leaders prevent Christian activity or request an interfaith event

Community tension

Applications by a religious group to build a religious centre

hen a religious community makes formal application to the Municipal Council to build a temple or mosque (or to buy and use an old church for this purpose) there is usually opposition from the (usually secular!) community. People consider that our heritage is Christian and they don't want other symbols being erected. Often there is the argument that Muslims won't let us build churches in their countries and Hindus are killing Christians in Nepal and India, all of which is true.

Nevertheless, as Christians we have no grounds for objecting to people pursuing their religious practices. If we don't want disused church buildings used for other religious activities then we should start a new Christian activity in the church building, or bulldoze down the building before selling it! We have no commitment to buildings and do not attach to buildings any spiritual meaning. On the other hand we recognise that buildings are symbols and we can be upset at symbols being used for other purposes.

We can justify objecting to an application to building next door to a church a building for a non-Christian religious purpose on the grounds of the confusion this may generate as to any relationship between the Christian community and the other religious group. We can also use the opportunity of an application for the erection of a building for another religious group to declare why Christians in the community are Christian. Any controversy that might arise could provide good media opportunity for declaring the basic truths of the gospel.

Opposition to Christian activity

There are occasions when a religious group seeks to prevent a Christian activity in a civic setting such as objecting to an ecumenical Service just prior to Easter or Christmas in a State school or Carols by Candlelight in the local park.

Christians should be free to argue their case on the grounds:

- we have the civil right to celebrate our faith so long as we do not disturb the community with high levels of noise (or break any other laws),

- pupils with a Christian heritage have the right to join together to learn about their faith and to give expression to it. Likewise those of other religious backgrounds may hold events for significant festivals for their own communities.

Any public celebrations we do organise should be pursued having in mind that some non-Christians may attend and thus we should plan to make clear the gospel at the event.

Request for inter-faith religious event

There are many different circumstances in a multi-cultural society which generate a desire for some religious activity which serves a mixed faith context. For instance, there can be

- a request from civic authorities for the leaders of religious groups to each offer a prayer at a special community ceremony;

- a request by a school for an inter-faith service so that the whole school can attend;
- a funeral service for a person with a mixed religious background or a memorial service for a large group of people who have been killed in a disaster, or
- a request for a leader in another religion to come to a church service and offer a prayer or read from that person's scriptures.

On the other hand, in a country where the majority follow another religion, a Christian pastor could be asked to read a passage from the bible or say a prayer at a State occasion or a memorial service.

In a multi-cultural society one is often under strong pressure to respond positively to a request for some type of inter-faith event. The foundational principles to have in mind in thinking through what is an appropriate response in the particular circumstances are:

a) Can it be clear that the Christians give praise to and pray to the Creator God who has been revealed in Jesus Christ who is *the* Word incarnate (not simply *a* word made flesh) i.e. the uniqueness of Jesus Christ and our faith rooted in him?

b) Can it be an opportunity to witness to Jesus Christ and his saving grace?

c) Is there likely to be confusion in the minds of those present as to whom one is praying?

These principles are basic. The answer to (a) and (b) needs to be *yes* and to (c) it needs to be *no* before any further consideration in undertaken. There may still be other factors to relate to before a decision is made, but one need not even ponder other matters if (a) and (b) are not *yes* and (c) is not *no*.

An invitation to take some part in an event organised by another religion can best be dealt with by reading an appropriate portion of the New Testament. If one is asked to pray at such an event, one's answer will depend on the prior answer to (c) above. If there are no Christians likely to be at such an event then there is no need to pray. If there will be Christians present then a prayer which clearly identifies God the Creator and Father of our Lord Jesus Christ and which is prayed in his name may be helpful.

Likewise a request for some religious leaders to each pray at a community event in our own country can be responded to by having in mind the above principles.

A request by a member of a bereaved family, for instance, to have a Hindu priest come and pray at the service because one of the bereaved's children is married to a Hindu, is best responded to by indicating that the service in the church is a Christian service, but that at the graveside or crematorium, after you have completed the prayers, the priest can say his prayer and then the body will be committed.

Another type of request is for a number of religious leaders to participate in a religious service e.g. at a school, a scout jamboree. The above principles also apply and the consequences of this are:

- you would not accept a piecing together of bits of readings and prayers to make a mosaic religious 'service', and if you were asked why you object you could point out that such an approach is syncretistic;

- you would not support such an event being held in a building which is identified as belonging to a particular religion as this would go against principle (c) above;

- you could be willing to conduct a Christian service at the conclusion of which leaders of other faiths would pray and/or read from their holy book (what is referred to as a 'serial multi-faith service');

- if a talk is to be given you would ask that each of the religious leaders give a three minute talk (so that you maintain the principles above); and

- you would prefer to have met with the other participants prior to the event so as to have an opportunity to talk with them about the purpose of the event and know that there will be mutual respect.

One doesn't seek to embarrass people of other faiths at such events, but one does need to be free to represent Jesus Christ and his saving grace. If this can be done in warmth and love, then your witness may well cause some to inquire further about the gospel.

Part III

Additional background material

A. Some global comparisons and significant dates

Some global statistics

In the year 2000			% of world population
World population	6,055,000,000	(6.06 billion)	
Christians (all kinds including nominal)	2,000,000,000	(2 billion)	33.0
Non-Christian (all other religions* and atheists)	4,055,000,000	(4.06 billion)	66.0
* Other religions			
Muslims	1,200,000,000	(1.2 billion)	20.0
Hindus	812,000,000	(812 million)	13.4
Chinese religion	(?)700,000,000	(700 million)	11.6
Buddhists	360,000,000	(360 million)	6.0
New religionists	102,000,000	(102 million)	1.7
Tribal religions (animism)	228,360,000	(228 million)	3.8
Shintoists	67,000,000	(67 million)	1.1
Sikhs	23,250,000	(23 million)	0.4
Jews	23,260,000	(23 million)	0.4

There is some overlap between these categories, for instance some people would be both Shintoists and Buddhists and some would be Chinese religionists and Buddhists. Taoists are not listed as most of them also follow another one of the Chinese or Japanese religions. There are a few minor religious groups not shown together with all who have no religious allegiance.[1]

Some significant dates in world history

Pre-history:	Animistic religions (the worship of spirits) and the mystery cults (like Mithraism which started in Persia and spread to Rome)
BC 2500	The first of the three pyramids (Khufu) at Giza was built
2300?	Abraham and his family migrated from Ur to the promised land via Egypt
2000?	The beginning of Hindu thought in the writing of the Vedas
1300?	The Exodus
1100 –	Phoenicians (coastal people of what now is Lebanon) develop trade routes across the Mediterranean to all the surrounding countries
1000 –	King David
922	Division of Israel into Northern and Southern Kingdoms
900	Phoenicians develop a 22 letter alphabet which becomes the basis for all European alphabets
800	The beginning of the development of urban society in Eastern Mediterranean countries (Greece, Asia Minor, Egypt)
750	Beginning of Greek and Phoenician colonisation around the Mediterranean due to developing trade
721	The fall of the Northern kingdom of Israel to Assyria
700	The first coin money, making trade much easier
587	Fall of Jerusalem to Nebuchadnezzar
580?	Lao-tzu was born in China and by 550 had brought into being the Taoist way of thinking built on earlier Chinese thought
560?	Buddha was born and by 500 had established a new 'religion'

A. Some global comparisons and significant dates

550?	Confucius was born in China
549	Cyrus of Persia conquered Babylon
499-478	The Persian wars, conquering Asia Minor and most of Greece
478	The Greeks conquered the Persians and the rise of the Greek 'golden age'
470-399	Plato
428-348	Socrates
336-323	Alexander the Great and the establishment of the Greek empire
264-146	Roman war against the remaining parts of the Phoenician colonisation (750-146) known as the Punic wars and against Greek colonisation (478-146)
146	Rome conquered the entire Mediterranean area
27	The Roman Emperor given greater powers because of disorder and civil wars in some of the colonies, with the result that the Emperor was given the title, *'Pontifex Maximus'*, which made him both the military commander and head of the state religion. Augustus was Emperor at the time and continued to be until AD 14, and so was Emperor when **Jesus was born**
AD 14-37	Tiberus, second Emperor of Rome
70	Destruction of the Temple in Jerusalem by the Romans
313-337	The reign of Constantine brought to an end the persecution of Christians. He set up his new kingdom's centre at Byzantium (a Greek colony), later to be renamed, Constantinople until it was conquered by the Turks in 1453, when it was renamed Istanbul.
622	Mohammad's flight to Medina – Year 1 in the Muslim calendar

630	Mohammad conquered Mecca and destroyed the 360 idols in the central temple; two years later he died
634	18,000 Muslims advanced on Palestine and Syria and by 636 overthrew the Byzantium and Persian armies. 40,000 Muslims marched through North Africa taking every city
711	Muslim Arabs annexed Spain and Sicily
781	Christianity was brought to central China through a Persian
1071	Seljuk Turks over ran most of Asia minor, but this new Turkish Empire lacked centralised power and the confusion and antagonism between the small Muslim principalities made it easy for the first Crusade to retake the 'Holy Lands'
1096	The first Crusade which succeeded in 1099 and set up Crusader Jerusalem for 88 years when it was retaken by the Muslims under Saladin
1219	Francis of Assisi visited the Sultan in Egypt and sought to bring to an end the Fifth Crusade
1299	A new Turkish dynasty – the Ottomans exploited the confused situation in Asia minor and conquered vast areas setting up the Ottoman Empire
1453	May 29, Constantinople surrendered to the Ottoman Empire. This Empire started to crumble in 1822 with the rebellion in Macedonia, but did not completely collapse until, with its ally Germany, it lost World War II
1456	The first printing of a major work – the Bible; at Mainz
1469-1539	Guru Nanak started Sikhism
1492	Christopher Columbus set out, August 3, from Portugal to look for Japan, but instead on March 15, 1493, found the islands now known as the West Indies

A. Some global comparisons and significant dates

1517	Beginning of the Reformation in Europe
1519	Cortés landed in Mexico and the following year the Spanish *conquistadors* took most of South America
1526	The first English New Testament
1549	Francis Xavier arrived in Japan with the gospel
1597	First martyrdoms in Japan – and the beginning of sustained persecution
1600	Formation of the East India Company
1733	First Moravian missionaries – went to Greenland
1728	First missionaries to India (Germans working with the Anglicans)
1751	First missionary to Africa – an Anglican to Ghana
1760	Beginning of the modern industrial 'revolution'
1789	French revolution
1792	William Carey – missionary to India (arrived 1793)
1799	Napoleon became First Consul of France and five years later declared himself Emperor of the French. The battle of Waterloo in June 1815, brought his rule to an end
1844	Karl Marx and Friedrich Engels met and set up the 'League of the Just' which soon after was renamed the 'Communist League'
1861	American Civil War
1839	Britain's Opium war with China
1894-95	Japan invaded north China
1907	Japan annexed Korea and established itself as the ruler of the Protectorate
1914-18	The Great War, later referred to as World War I. End of the Ottoman empire which was carved up into new Arabian/Middle East states

1917	The Russian revolution. Lenin lead the first ever Communist Government
1931	Japan conquered the northern part of China
1937	March 7, Hitler ordered his army to march into the Rhineland
1939	September 3, World War II started
1941	December 7, Japan bombed Pearl Harbour and another war engulfed the Pacific
1945	June 26, the signing of the Charter bringing into being the United Nations (replacing the League of Nations set up at the end of the First World War)

---

1 Figures are based on David Barrett's statistics published annually in the January issue of *The International Bulletin of Missionary Research*.

B. List of countries/regions with religious groups in population

It is not safe to predict a person's religious background just by knowing the country from which they come. However, it may help to be aware of the different religions that are represented in each country. One needs to also bear in mind that even when a person says they are of 'X' faith, that their own personal doctrinal views and devotional practices may be very different from the mainline expressions of that faith. So be careful not to make assumptions. Nevertheless, facts about the country of interest in this list may help you to be sensitive and ready for a range of answers.

Religious groups in each country are listed in order of statistical significance.

Africa

Countries will not be separately listed since a generalisation can be made, but exceptions are then noted.

Most countries have a Muslim presence and those north of the Sahara have a Muslim majority. All west African countries have a major Muslim presence.

All countries south of the Sahara have a Christian presence which can be categorised under the headings of Catholic, Anglican, Protestant (which includes Pentecostal) and indigenous Christian churches.

All countries have some people following traditional African religions (these are animistic religions).

Some countries have a majority Christian population, such as Kenya, Zambia, Zimbabwe and South Africa.

Note especially:

East African countries have Indian/Pakistani migrant groups (some have been there for many generations) and these groups are either of a Muslim or Hindu tradition.

Of the 'horn of Africa' countries, Djibouti, is 90% Muslim and Somalia 99% Muslim.

Egypt has an estimated 8 million Christians in a total population of 64 million, although government statistics regard the number of Christians as being very much smaller. The Christian presence dates back to the first century AD and tradition has it that Mark brought the Gospel to Egypt. The two largest groups of Christians are the Coptic Orthodox and Evangelical Coptic (Presbyterian). There are small congregations of other Eastern Orthodox, Anglican and Protestants.

The Sudan had 2 million Christians mainly in the south of the country, but many of them have become refugees in surrounding countries because of the Islamic attack on the south since the mid 1980's.

Ethiopia has a majority Christian population. Just over half are members of the Ethiopian Orthodox Church which dates back to AD 332. There are small numbers of Protestants and Catholics. Nearly a third of the population is Muslim and around 10% of the population follow traditional tribal religions (animism).

West Asia, Arabia and the Middle East

Afghanistan: Majority are Muslims – most are Sunnis, with some Shi'ites or other sects. There are some 100,000 Indians living in Afghanistan, some of whom are Hindus or Sikhs.

Bahrain: Most are Sunni Muslims, some are Shi'ites. There are some Christians, the Gospel having come to Bahrain in the 4th century.

Cyprus: – Turkish: All the Turkish Cypriots are Sunni Muslim.
– Greek: All the Greek Cypriots are Christian; all but for a few are Greek Orthodox.

Kuwait: Most are Sunni Muslims. There are a few Christians.

Iran: Majority are Shi'ite Muslim. A small number are Baha'is, or Parsees (i.e. Zoroastrians). There are also some Christians including Armenian Orthodox, Anglicans and Protestants.

Iraq: Majority are Muslim, just over half being Shi'ites, the others Sunnis. Christians have been there since the first century AD. The oldest church is the Assyrian Orthodox and there are some Anglican and Protestant communities. There are some small syncretistic groups which include a mix of Jewish, Zoroastrian and Christian elements.

Israel: Majority of the Israeli population are secular Jews. Those who are committed to the Jewish faith are politically very active. There are a small number of Christian Jews referred to as Messianic Jews. Within the State of Israel there is also an ethnic Arabic population, many of whom are Muslim, and a significant number are Christians (Anglican, Catholic and Protestant).

Jordan: Majority is Sunni Muslim. Five per cent of the population is Christian.

Lebanon: Half the population is Christian (Maronites and a small Protestant church), the other half Muslim. Half of these are Sunnis and the others are made up of Shi'ite, Druze and other Muslim sects.

Oman, Qatar, the Emirates and Yemen: Majority are Sunni Muslim. There are very few Christians.

Saudi Arabia: All are Sunni Muslims.

Syria: The majority is Sunni Muslim. Christianity dates back to the days of St Paul and today around 7% are Christians. The Greek Orthodox Church is the largest Christian community, but there are other Orthodox and a Catholic church, as well as a small number of Protestants.

Turkey: The majority is Sunni Muslim. There is a small Jewish community and there are a few shamanists. Christianity dates back to the visits of St Paul. A number of Orthodox Churches still have a presence.

Asia – Indian Subcontinent

Bangladesh: The majority is Muslim. There are a small number of Hindus and Christians.

Bhutan: The majority is Buddhist. Those who were originally from Nepal or India (about 24% of the population) are Hindus. There is a handful of Christians.

India: The majority is Hindu (79%), there is a significant Muslim presence (10%) and a less significant Christian presence (3%). There is a smaller number of Sikhs (2%) and Zoroastrians. The Indian state of Sikkim regards Buddhism as the official religion, but this has a following of only 27% of the population. The Baha'is are growing in Sikkim. In the states of Kerala and Nagaland, there is a very significant Christian presence.

Maldives: All are Muslim.

Nepal: The majority is Hindu. There is a rapidly growing Christian population and a small number of Buddhists and Muslims.

Pakistan: The majority is Sunni Muslim, with the Ahmadis sect being the largest sect (3%). Christian presence dates back to the 8th century but today is only 2% of the population. There are also some Hindus and some Parsees (Zoroastrians).

Sri Lanka: The majority is Buddhist (all of whom are Singhalese, 67 %). There are significant numbers of Hindus (mainly among the Tamils, 16%), Christians (7.5%) and Muslims (7.5%).

Tibet: All are Buddhist apart from a handful of Christians.

Asia – East and South

Brunei: All the Malays are Muslim. Some of the tribal people are animists and some are Christian. Chinese ethnics are Buddhists or

B. List of countries/regions with religious groups in population

Chinese religionists with a few Christians. There are some Baha'is and most of the Indian ethnics are Hindu.

Cambodia/Kampuchea: The majority is Buddhist. There are some animists, Muslims and a few Christians.

China, Peoples Republic of: The majority of those born in the past 40 years have grown up with no religious teaching. But many would still worship their ancestors and so could be described as Chinese religionists (see Chapter 12 for more detail). There is a growing number of Christians; estimates vary from 7 million to 50 million (i.e. 0.6–4% of the whole population).

The special region of Hong Kong: The majority are Chinese religionists, but at least 10% of the population are Christian (Catholic, Anglican, Protestant). It is estimated that 15% have no religion.

China, Republic of (Taiwan): Half the population is Chinese religionist. Most of the others are Buddhists apart from the 9% who are Christians (Protestant, Catholic and Anglican).

Indonesia: Three-quarters of the population are Muslim. These are mainly Sunnis but many are 'folk-Muslims'. The people of the Indonesian island of Bali are Hindus. There is a significant Christian presence (12%). Quite a number are animists (5%) or Chinese religionists (1.5%).

Japan: Sixty three per cent follow traditional Japanese religions, 23% follow the new religions, at least 10% have no religion and around 1.5% are Christians (Catholic, Protestant and Anglican).

Laos: Around 60% are Buddhists, 34% are animists and 2% are Christians (mostly Catholics and a few Protestants). The others are Chinese religionists or atheists.

Korea – South: One quarter of the population is shamanist and another quarter is Christian (Catholic, Anglican and Protestants). Around 16% is Buddhist and 13% Confucianist.

Korea – North: Most have had no exposure to any religion since the mid 1950's. There are a handful of Christians.

Macau: The majority (60%) is Chinese religionist, 30% is Christian (Catholic, Anglican and Protestant).

Malaysia: The Malays (half the population) are by law Muslim. Some of the tribal people of Sarawak and Sabah are also Muslim but most are Christian. The non-Malays who are of Indian origin are Hindus, Sikhs or Muslim. The majority of the non-Malays are of Chinese origin and they follow Chinese religions apart from those who are Christians.

Philippines: The majority is Catholic Christian. Some Christians are Protestants or Episcopalians (Anglican). Six per cent of the population is Muslim (mainly in the south) and 15% is Chinese religionist.

Singapore: The population is made up of a majority of Chinese, half of whom follow Chinese religions or no religion at all. There is a growing number of Christians among the Chinese and among the Indian population. The other Indians are Hindu, Muslim or Sikh. There is a small Muslim Malay population.

Thailand: The majority of the population is Buddhist. There is a small enclave of Muslims in the south. Some 4% of the population are Christian.

Vietnam: Just over half the population is Buddhist. Some 20% regard themselves as atheists. Some 15% follow animistic or Chinese folk religions. Around 8% are Christians (Catholics and Protestants).

Europe – West

Christianity dominates these countries nominally. Due to migration there is a growing number of Muslims and a small number of Hindus and Chinese religionists.

Europe – East

Most of the population in what was the former USSR has been referred to as the CIS, but is now increasingly being called Eurasia have had little opportunity to learn about any religion since 1917 and so would be atheists. But the Christians have maintained some witness and since 1991, a growing number of young people have been going to Sunday School and youth groups. Most of the Christians are Orthodox, with some Protestants and some Catholics.

The following States have a majority of the population at least nominally Muslim: Azerbaijan, Chechyna, Dagastan, Kazakhstan, Kirghizia, Tajikistan, Tatarstan, Turkmenistan and Uzbekistan. There are Muslim enclaves in some of the other countries. There is a renewed interest in Islam in these countries, assisted by the distribution of the Qur'an and the building of Mosques through funds from Saudi Arabia and Turkey.

There are Buddhist enclaves in the Central Asia republics.

The Eastern European countries have a significant Orthodox and Catholic presence.

The ethnic groups that were joined together as Yugoslavia at the end of World War I, are either Orthodox, Catholic or Muslim. Albania, on the western border of Yugoslavia, had all Christians killed in the 1940's. There is now a growing number people attending the newly opened churches.

Latin America and West Indies

West Indies: The majority is Christian (Protestants, Anglicans and Catholics). Some follow African animistic religions.

Latin American countries: The majority is Catholic with a growing number of Protestants. Uruguay has a very large proportion of its population regarding themselves as atheists. There are some followers of traditional animistic religions. In Suriname there are some Hindus and Muslims among the Indian and Javanese ethnics.

South Pacific

Fiji: All Fijian ethnics are Christians. The Indian Fijians are Hindu or Muslim with some being Christians.

Melanesian countries (PNG, Solomon Is, Vanuatu & New Caledonia): The majority are Christians with the others being animists.

Micronesian countries: All are Christian.

Polynesian countries: All are Christian except for a handful of Baha'is, and most of the Chinese ethnics living in these islands are either Chinese religionists or Christians.

Information for this Resource Unit has been gleaned from various sources including some government publications and from David B. Barrett (ed.), *World Christian Encyclopedia*, OUP.

C. Further reading and resources

To use with enquirers

Two Ways to Live (also a small leaflet bible study) St Matthias & Anglican Press Australia

Christianity Explained, Scripture Union Australia

What is a Christian? Anglican Press Australia

To give to Muslims

The Prophets and the Word (obtainable from Box 96, Pymble, 2073)

The Gospel of Jesus Christ according to John, Bible Society Australia

For evangelism training

Abbott, Stephen. *Everyday Evangelism* (Student's book, Trainers Manual and Video), Dept of Evangelism, St Andrew's House, Sydney

Anderson, M. A series of small books on what to say about various biblical issues to Muslims, (obtainable from PO Box 129, Belmore, NSW 2192)

Chapman, John. C. *Know and Tell the Gospel*, Matthias Media, 1998

Corney, Peter. *The Gospel and the Growing Church*, AIO, 1988

Dennett, Bill. *Sharing the Good News with Muslims* (obtainable from Box 96, Pymble, 2073)

For new resources look up www.christianity.net.au

Further background material on other religions

The World's Religions, A Lion Handbook, 1982

Musk, Bill. *The Unseen Face of Islam*, MARC, 1989 (all about folk Islam)

Nazir-Ali, Michael. *Islam – A Christian Perspective*, Paternoster, 1983

Chapman, Colin. *Cross and Crescent: Responding to the challenge of Islam*, IVP, 1995

Nickel, Gordon D. *Peaceable Witness Among Muslims*, Herald Press, 1999

Hughes, Philip J. (ed) A series on Religious Community Profiles on each of the major religions in Australia, AGPS 1996-8

The persecuted church

Any history of the early church will provide some information about the persecution of the early centuries e.g.

Bruce, F.F. *The Spreading Flame*, Paternoster, 1958

Smith, M.A. *The Church Under Siege*, IVP, 1976

Walker, G.S.M. *The Growing Storm*, Paternoster, 1961

For some current stories, see

Claydon, Robyn. *Doors are for Walking Through*, SPCKA, 1998 (stories of people who have become Christians with teaching)

Chenu, Bruno and others. *The Book of Christian Martyrs*, SCM, 1988

Gulshan, Esther. *The Torn Veil* and *Beyond the Veil*, Marshall Pickering, 1990/92 (story of a Muslim convert)

Challenging reading about mission

Green, Michael. *Evangelism through the Local Church*, Hodder, 1991

Nazir-Ali, Michael. *From Everywhere to Everywhere – A World View of Christian Mission*, Collins, 1991

Netland, Harold A. *Dissonant Voices – Religious Pluralism and the Question of Truth*, Wm. B. Eerdmans, 1992

Newbigin, Lesslie. *Foolishness to the Greeks*, Wm. B. Eerdmans, 1986
_____. *The Gospel in a Pluralist Society*, Wm. B. Eerdmans, 1989

O'Brien, Peter (ed). *God's Mission and Ours*, CMS Australia, 1999 (this has separate study questions and an introductory video)

Wright, Chris. *What's So Unique About Jesus*, MARC, 1990

A most helpful book about ministry among the Aborigines

Harris, John. *We Wish We'd Done More*, Open Book, 1998

Books on the New Age

Albrecht, Mark C. *Reincarnation: A Christian Critique of a New Age Doctrine*, IVP, 1982

Groothius, Douglas R. *Confronting the New Age*, IVP, 1988

_____. *Unmasking the New Age*, IVP, 1986

Miller, Elliot. *A Crash Course on the New Age*, Baker Book House/ Monarch, 1990

Study Guide

Chapter 1

Why witness?

1. God has communicated with humanity in various ways. What and how has he communicated according to the following passages?

    Genesis 15:1 ....

    Exodus 3:1-6 ....

    1 Samuel 3:10-14 ....

    Isaiah 1:1-2 ....

    Jeremiah 11:6; 6:1-11 ....

    Luke 1:22, 26; 2:8-14 ....

    Luke 4:1 ....

    Romans 8:26-27 ....

    Hebrews 1:1 ....

2. What are three of the most important reasons for God to reveal himself to humanity?

    Genesis 19:3-6 ....

    ....

    Isaiah 6:3 ....

    ....

Study Guide

Luke 4:18-19 ....

....

3. The Israelites were called out of slavery to be God's people and to be

 .... (Isaiah 42:6, 49:6).

 Can you find similar statements in the Gospels?
 (A concordance will be helpful.)

 ....

 ....

4. We and all humanity have a creation identity, namely

 .... (Genesis 1:26-27)

5. This has been spoilt by .... (Genesis 3)

6. Those who have accepted Christ's free gift of forgiveness and eternal life have a redeemed identity.

 - Read 1 Peter 2:1-10
 - List below each of the picture words used in this passage about those who belong to God:

 .... (verse   )

 .... (verse   )

 .... (verse   )

 .... (verse   )

 .... (verse   )

7. Peter in his letter has stated very definitely that we have been reinstated as 'God's own people' (1 Peter 2:9) and that we are very precious to him (verse 4). This redeemed identity gives rise to a responsibility, namely

    .... (1 Peter 2:9b).

8. The church is the body of Christ' (1 Corinthians 12:27), the temple of the Holy Spirit (1 Corinthians 3:16), the people of God. God has called the church into being and empowered it to be a distinctive people representing God in the midst of his creation. What are some of the different ways we can represent God in our world?

    For instance

    By showing God's caring love (Luke 4:18-19) ....

    ....

    By demonstrating positive values (Galatians 5:19-24) ....

    ....

    By challenging wrong social ideas (Philemon 8-19) ....

    ....

    Some other ways are ....

    ....

    ....

    ....

    ....

    ....

Study Guide

Chapter 2

Objections to Christian witness

1. Jesus himself made it clear that we are responsible to share the Good News. For instance, read the following records of his Commission. Next to each reference below, write the command words in each text:

   - Matthew 28:19-20 ....
   - Mark 16:15 ....
   - Luke 24:47 ....
   - John 17:18; 20:21 ....

2. The Gospel passages above may be a record of just one or two occasions when Jesus instructed his disciples about the future. But Acts 1:8 records Christ's words on a separate occasion ie. after the resurrection and just prior to his ascension. With this commission recorded in Acts comes a promise which is

   ....

   ....

3. The Holy Spirit is the active agent in our work of witnessing. What are some of the other promises we have about the work of the Holy Spirit that can make us keen to tell others about the gospel? See the following passages:

   Romans 8:9-11 ....

   ....

   Galatians 5:22-25 ....

   ....

Ephesians 1:13-14 ....

....

4. Read Romans 8:1-2 and 37-39. What practical effect do the assurances that these verses convey have on the way you live your life?

....

....

....

Chapter 3

How the major religions' view Christianity

1. The 'Christian' west has made positive contributions to the world that many in less privileged countries long to benefit from. List some of these life-enhancing contributions below the examples given.

   - Medical advances
   - The spread of education
   - ....
   - ....
   - ....
   - ....
   - ....
   - ....

2. In the eyes of many, the west has also been destructive of important life values. Discuss the image that the western world has projected through

- colonialism
- wars
- economic exploitation and any other ways you can identify.

3. Discuss how you think people in your neighbourhood or workplace see Christianity, for example:

- one religion among many
- a religion that is 'western' (European) in culture and tends to wipe out other cultures and traditions
- the religion of aggressive, warmongering nations
- an unloving, judging religion
- a value system that encourages people to help others
- a religion that has in the past permitted oppression e.g. slavery and apartheid
- a religion that provides a helpful moral basis for living
- a value system that urges people to love others but fails to bring about that result

Is your local church doing anything to promote negative perceptions of Christianity? In what ways could it do more than it is currently doing to promote positive perceptions? Discuss.

4. How was Christianity viewed by the Ephesians, as recorded in Acts 19:23-41, and was their view correct?

5. Imagine you are talking with a person who has been brought up in another religion (and/or a non-western culture) about becoming a Christian. How would you deal with this person's fears about:

- the negative influences of western society, which he or she sees as a product of Christianity

....

....

....

- the likely reaction of the immediate family if one of their number decides to become a Christian

....

....

....

- breaking with traditional family attitudes and values

....

....

....

Chapter 4

More than one way to witness

The gospel in your life:

1. Read 1 Thessalonians 1

    List the different ways that the gospel was communicated in this chapter:

    v.5 ....

    ....

v.6 ....

....

v.7 ....

....

List the consequences of the gospel when it is communicated:

v.8 ....

v.9 ....

v.10 ....

Now describe some of the ways that the gospel is being communicated, or could be, to new migrants in your district.

....

....

....

2. Read Acts 17:16-27. Note that Paul proclaimed the gospel both to people of his own religious/cultural background and to those with the entirely different background.

   Tick any words below that best describe Paul's approach to people in v.33

   ____ cunning

   ____ affirming

   ____ paternalistic

   ____ sensitive

   ____ manipulative

   ____ relevant

Discuss some ways this model of communicating can be used today.

....

....

The gospel in action

3. One of the consequences of being part of God's family is that we should reflect the character of God by helping those in need ('good deeds'). Jesus himself made this clear in Matthew 25:31-46.

    Discuss some of the ways in which good deeds can be:

    - a bridge to the proclamation of the gospel

    - a partner in the act of proclamation

    - a demonstration of the reality of the gospel, for instance, in changing lives

    Is your church helping people in the district in some significant way? If not, does the group have any suggestions to make?

    ....

    ....

    ....

Chapter 5

Not on your own

1. Identify the different ways our relationship with God – Father, Son and Holy Spirit is taught in Paul's letter to the Ephesians.

    1: 5 ....

Study Guide

    10 ....

    13-14 ....

      22-23 ....

  2: 1 ....

     5 ....

     6 ....

     10 ....

     18 ....

     19 ....

     20 ....

     21 ....

     22 ....

  3: 19 ....

  4: 15 ....

     24 ....

     30 ....

As you look down this list you can see clearly that Christ has made us a very important part of God's family. How should this fact affect us as we think about reaching out to others?

....

....

2. Identify the different ways the members of God's family relate to one another as taught in Ephesians.

  2: 19 ....

   20 ....

   21 ....

  3: 10 ....

   17 ....

   18-19 ....

  4: 3 ....

   4-7 ....

   11-14 ....

   31 ....

   32 ....

  5: 1-2 ....

   19 ....

   21 ....

New Christians are to become part of this family, the church. Is your church welcoming, particularly to people who have a different cultural/ethnic background? What could you do to help your church become more understanding and more welcoming?

....

....

3. A fundamental ingredient in our fellowship with God and with each other is that we know Christ. This means we know who he is and that he is at work in us and in the world. For this reason, Jesus instructed his disciples, saying, 'go therefore and make disciples...teaching them to observe all that I have taught you...'

  Paul pursues this emphasis on teaching and discipling. For instance, read Paul's prayer in Colossians 1:9-14.

Study Guide

a) In this passage Paul prays for particular results as the Colossians continue to grow in understanding. What are these results?

....
....
....
....
....

b) Suggest ways the members of your study group can help one another to grow in 'wisdom and spiritual understanding'.

....
....
....

Chapter 6

Principles for cross-cultural evangelism

Know what you believe

1. Read Ephesians 2:1-10

   a) List below what this passage tells us about ourselves before Christ's saving work was applied to our lives

   v.1b ....

   v.2 ....

   v.3 ....

   v.5 ....

b) List below what this passage tells about what God has done for us

v.1a and v.5 ....

v.4 ....

v.6 ....

v.7 ....

v.8 ....

v.10 ....

Review the points listed above and discuss how you might tell someone who is not a Christian about the message of Ephesians 2:8

Start where your hearer is

2. The children of Israel were taught to care about the foreigners/ strangers/sojourners living among them. (Look up a concordance to check out these references.) What motivates us to care about the migrants in our midst?

....

Pray

3. Christians are called to pray for one another (Ephesians 6:18). Paul provides several models of specific things to ask for when praying for others. Read one of these, in Ephesians 3:14-21 and list below the points he makes:

....

....

....

....

....

....
....
....
....

Discuss a plan of action to enable your congregation to pray more earnestly for one another and for new members.

Have a spirit of humility and be willing to listen

4. Read Acts 10:24-33

    a) Why did Peter cross this ethnic boundary so easily?

    ....
    ....

    b) Note Peter's question in v.29 and list below what Cornelius expected of Peter.

    ....
    ....

    c) Share any experiences you may have had of God already at work in preparing a person you have befriended to want to know more about Jesus.

5. Review the principles for cross-cultural evangelism and discuss what further action the group could take to enable members to grow in confidence in making contact with a migrant family.

Chapter 7

Making contact

Paul provides us with some helpful examples of how to make contact with those who have never heard the good news.

1. Read Acts 17:1-9

a) What did Paul have in common with those he talked to in Thessalonica (v.1)?

   ....

   ....

b) What was it in Paul's teaching that annoyed some of the Jews?

   ....

   ....

2. Read 1 Thessalonians 2:1-12

a) What motivated Paul to proclaim the good news about Jesus the Christ (the Messiah) vv.3-4

   ....

b) Paul uses picture words to describe the way he related to the Thessalonians (vv.7-8 and 11-12). These are

   ....

   Discuss each of these two ways to relate to others and how they may apply to you.

c) Paul's personal life had come under some scrutiny and so he reminds the people of what they know about him, which is

   v.2 ....

   v.3 ....

v.4 ....

v.5 ....

v.6 ....

v.9 ....

v.10 ....

Your life is under scrutiny by those who live close to you, even sometimes by a neighbour. Are there some aspects of your life that need to change? What steps can you take to keep growing and become more and more like Christ?

....

....

....

d) In v.9 Paul says he both worked hard (see Acts 18:3, 20-34) and preached the gospel. Why do you think it was important to remind the Thessalonians of his income-earning work

....

....

3. Identify some of the migrant families in your district and discuss ways in which you and your group can make contact with one or more of these.

....

....

....

4. Discuss

    a) how you would identify a non-Christian's understanding of the Divine, and

    b) how you would seek to lead such a person on from this understanding to the point where you can talk about what God has told us about himself and how he wants us to respond.

index

A

aboriginal language, research on 125, 130n
    missionaries and 130
aborigines, Australian 125-130
    Christian 127, 128
    'dreamtime motif' 126, 129
    integrated view of life 125, 126
    loss of identity and today 127
Abraham 10, 66
ahl al kitab, *see* Qur'an
American Civil War 30
American Indians, *see* Nature religions
ancestor worship, *see also* Confucianism 59, 109, 110
Angra Mainyu 133
Animism, 75, 117, 163
Arian controversy 67
Arjan, Guru 96
Artemis 14
ashrams 89, 142
atman, 84 *see* Hinduism
atheist 59, 60
Avesta, *see* Zoroastrianism

B

Bab *see* Baha'i
Baha'i 131-2
    on God 132
    views 132

Barrett, David 162, 170
Beatles 142
Besant, Annie 141 *see also* New Age movement
Bhagavad Gita 83, 90
Bhakti movement 85, 88
    deities, development of 85
Bible 19, 34, 37, 76, 77, 78, 79, 80
Bible Study group 45, 139, 147
Bonaparte, Napoleon 30
Brahman 84, 85, 93, 96 *see also* Hinduism
Buddha 22, 25, 95, 99, 100, 102, 103, 104, 105, 106, 108n
    rejection of mortification 99
Buddhism, Buddhists 22, 54, 87, 89, 94n, 99-108, 109, 112, 113, 118, 133, 141, 142, 143
    see also Ch'an, Mahayana or Northern, Theravada or Southern, Nichiren Shoshu & Zen Buddhism
    on Christianity 104
    similarities with 106
    dharma 100, 106
    ethical behaviour in 103
    on suffering 106-7
    teachings 102, 103
        Four Noble Truths 102; Noble Eightfold Path 102
        traditions of, different 99, 100
        types of 99, 100
        Mayayana 99: on nirvana 103; Theravada 99-100
            caste system 59, 85, 86, 91, 93, 95, 99, 102
            and groupings 86

C

Ch'an Buddhism 112-13
    in Japan 118

on individual 113

'interior light' 113

Chinese religion 109-116, 57

teachings drawn from Buddhism 112-13

Christ, *see* Jesus Christ

Christendom 39, 67

Christian heritage 135

2000 year old churches 135-6

continuity of historical churches 135

Christians, Christianity 10, 11, 13, 16, 18-23, 25-31, 33, 34, 37, 38, 40-42, 44, 46-49, 51-54, 58, 60, 65-71, 72, 74-79, 87-89, 90-93, 97, 98, 104-105, 114, 115, 120-122, 126-129, 136-140, 141-142, 147, 150

events making decisive impact on 26

faith, central truths 51-2

growth under persecution 27

identity of 10-11

facts related to 11

major religions' views, factors influencing 25-6

in non-European countries 25-6

negative perceptions of, due to 29-33

colonialism, history of 31-2; economic exploitation 33; moral decadence 33; prejudice 33; wars 29-31

Church 18, 22, 25-29, 39, 43, 46, 57, 136, 139, 140

belonging, sense of 25-6

caring compassion and 28

integrated program of a growing 44

and mission 22

Church Universal 17

colonialism 31-2, 67-8

economic exploitation 33

history of 31-2

and third world, impression of 31, 33

communication 55
community caring program 45
compassion 20
Conference of British Missionary Societies 34
confrontation 58
Confucianism 59, 109-12, *see also* ancestor worship
Confucius 59, 109-11, 115
    ancestor worship 110
    ethical principles 111
congregation 39, 43
    choosing a 137-9
    Christian communities, appreciating others' 139-40
    concerted prayers and mission program 44
    designing a program 43-7
    evangelism training 43, 45
    newcomers, attracting and caring for 46-7
    pastoral care 43, 45, 49
        developing network 45
    teaching program 47-9
    preaching program, units of 47-9
    training in 43
Constantine, Emperor 27, 68, 136
Conversion 18-19, 21, 86
Creator God 10, 60-1, 92, 95, 100, 107, 121, 153, 154
Cross, Christ's work on 11, 20-22, 51
Crusades 29-30, 67-8

D

Dalai Lama 103, 108n
determinism, *see* Hinduism
dialogue 55, 72
    body language 55
Divine justice 20

Divine Light Mission 142
Divine power 59
dogmatism 22
'dreamtime, 125, 126-7, 129

E

East India Company 30, 87
Elkin, Professor A.P.
    research on aborigines 125, 126, 130n
English, Druids *see* Nature religions
Enlightenment 18th century 53
environmentalists 125
Ephesians 13, 14, 37, 48, 80, 107, 115, 147
eternal life 22
evangelism 9-10, 40
    cross-cultural 51-2
    engaging in, reasons for 10-16
        as matter of identity 10-13
        as matter of motivation 13-14
    friendship 13, 40
    training 45
evangelistic calling 18
extended family 14, 15, 137

F

First World War 17, 30, 68
Five Classics 109
French Revolution 30
friendship evangelism 40
fung-shui, 'science of' 112

G

Gandhi, Mahatma 89
Gita, see Bhagavad Gita 90
God's grace 18
Gnosticism 144
Golden Temple 96
gospel 5, 18, 23, 42, 58, 61, 128, 135
    in action 42
    damage to 29-33
    demonstration of true 34
    discipline involved in 51-5
    through friendship 13, 57-61
    digging deeper 59; introducing question of faith 58; one-to-one conversation 58-9
    global 18-23
    gossiping of, principles 39, 51-5
        know what you believe 51; start where your hearer is 52; cover with prayer 53; spirit of humility 54; willing to listen 54
    imperatives for motivation to make known 11
        a changed life 12; the great commandment 13; Great Commission 12; loving Jesus 12
    message, uniqueness of 51-2
    in word 38
        ways to witness through 38-42
        declared 40-41; friendship 40; liturgy 39; media reach 41
        world events and spread of 26-9
            Christian church, sense of belonging 26; Church, role of 26-9;
            cities of Greek and Roman Empire 26; Greek language and 26; Roman law 26
    in your life 37-8
        spiritual regimen 38
Gospels 39, 66, 79, 80

Great Commandment 13
    Love, meaning of 12
Great Depression 30
Greek Empire 26, 27, 31
Gulf War 69, 70
Guru Granth (*Granth Sahib*) 96, 98
Guru Nanak 95, 160
    views of 95-6

H

Hadith 70-72, 74
Hafiz 71
Hare Krishna 142
Hick, John 19, 23n
Hinduism, Hindus 21, 30, 54, 83-94, 95, 96, 97, 99, 133-4, 135, 141, 146, 154
    Balinese and 86, 94n
    on Christians 87
    determinism 84, 89
    divine 21, 59, 87, 88, 89
    notable gods 85, 94n
    and Jainism 133-4
    rebirth and karma 84, 85, 88, 89, 92, 93, 99, 133, 143
    reincarnation 21, 84, 85, 86, 91, 92, 143
    renaissance in 88-90
    Three Pathways (*margas*) 84
        Bhakti marga 85, 88; and deities 85; Janan marga 84, 88; Karma marga 85, 91
Holy Land 30, 67, 81n
Holy Spirit 11, 12, 22, 23, 32, 34, 38, 41, 43, 52, 53, 54, 55, 58, 73, 79, 80, 87, 93, 107, 116, 126, 128, 132, 137, 139, 147, 148
Homeopathy 44
humanism, new forms of 143
'human potential movement' 144

I

ideology 25, 145
immigrants, major problems of 14, 52
    and cultural identity 52
International Bulletin of Missionary Research, The 162n
injil 66
Isaiah, Prophet 10, 11, 73
Islam 19, 20, 27, 28, 65-81, 89, 95, 97, 132, 135, 136
    five pillars of 71-2
    God's revelation, progression of 65-6, 72
    groups within 73-5
    intellectuals 74; legalists 74; Muslim folk religion 74; Shia's 73, 131; Sunnis 73, 74
    meaning of 65
    Shari'a Law 70, 71, 74, 75, 126
    Code 70
Israel, Israelists 10, 11, 19, 23, 60, 129

J

Jainism 133
    and Hinduism 133
    on holy life and meaning of 133-4
    24 Jinas 134
Janan marga 84, 88
Japan
    population 120
    resistance to pursue religion 120
Japanese religions 117-123
    ancient religions 117-119
    loyalty to Emperor 118, 121
    modern religious movements 119-21
    secular nature of 120-1

Jerusalem 12, 67, 81n, 135
Jesus Christ 5, 9, 11, 12, 13, 14, 17, 18, 19, 20, 21, 22, 26, 27, 34, 35, 37, 38, 39, 40, 41, 43, 44, 45, 46, 51, 53, 54, 55, 58, 60, 66, 67, 72, 73, 76, 77, 79, 80, 81, 87, 88, 89, 91, 92, 93, 94, 97, 105, 106, 107, 108, 115, 116, 122, 126, 128, 130, 132, 135, 136, 138, 139, 147, 148

    anonymous presence of 21, 22

    as God and Saviour 11, 21, 22

    and Great Commission 12, 23

    logos, in form of 18

    loving 12

    ministry, purpose of 19

    revelation of God in 54

    and salvation 80

    as way to Father 18, 19

Jews 11, 14, 20, 21, 22, 72, 132

Jihad 73

Judaism 22, 74

Judaea 12

John 12, 19, 27, 53, 66, 80, 81, 87, 92, 115

K

kami *see* Shintoism

karma 88, 89, 91, 107, 143 *see also* Hinduism

karma marga 85, 91

khalsa 96

Knitter, Paul 18, 23n

Koories, *see* aborigines

Kriol language, *see* aborigines

L

Lao-tzu 111

Lenin 30

Linssen, Robert 113, 116n
Lister, Joseph 34
liturgy 39
love of God 10
Luke 12, 13, 22, 48, 79, 80

M

MacLaine, Shirley 146
Maharishi, Mahesh Yogi 142
    Transcendental Meditation 142
Mahavira Vardhamana, *see* Jainism
Mancius 110
Mar Thoma 88
Mark 12, 13, 27, 80, 135
Marx, Karl, Marxism 30, 75
Mary 72, 73,
Matthew 12, 13, 22, 48, 80, 107, 138, 150
Maya 86
Mayayana Buddhism 99, 103
Mecca (*Haj*) 72, 73
Medina 66
Meditation 84
Megatrends 142 *see also* New Age movement
Migrants 135-6
    Christian heritage of 135
    first generation 136-7
    making contacts with 52, 57-61
    facing prejudice 33
Mirza Hasayn Ali Nurf (Baha'i) 131
Mission and evangelism 17-18
mission program 43-4
modern missionary movement 34
Mohammad (Prophet) 21, 30, 65, 66, 71, 72, 74, 80

Moltmann, Jürgen 81n

monks 89, 105

Moses 10, 66, 71, 83

Muhammad, Sayyid Ali (Bab) *see also* Baha'i 131

multi-culturalism 9

Muslim folk religion 74-5

Muslims 19, 21, 28, 29, 31, 33, 53, 54, 65-81, 94n, 95, 126, 132, 133

    views of Christians, sources of 65-71

    contact between Christians and 66-71; after death of Mohammad 66;

    colonialism and imperialism 66-8; commercial media and tourist contact 33, 70; crusades 67-68;

    discovery of oil 69; Gulf War 69, 70; Quran 65-6

    on Jesus 72

    lifestyle 77

    meaning of 65

    progression of God's revelation 65-6

mysticism *see* also New Age movement 142, 145

N

Naisbett 141

Namaste 146

Napoleonic wars 30

Nasr, Professor Seyyed 71, 81n

Nature religions, 144

Nestorian 66

New Age movement 89, 141-150

    attitudes, range of 142-4

        astrology 143; eastern spirituality/mysticism 141, 142 ; ecology 144; human potential movement 144; Nature or folk religions 144; occult 143; reincarnation 143; Hindu and Buddhist belief 89, 143

differences with other religions 146-7
   reasons for turning to 145-6
   self as God, views on 146
      consequences of 146
New Agers 144, 145, 146, 147
   steps for discussion with 148-9
New Consciousness movement 142
New Testament 65, 72, 73, 77, 92, 98, 105
Newton, Isaac 34
Newton, John 34
Nyoongahs, *see* Aborigines
Nichiren Shoshu Buddhism 119
nirvana, meaning of and origin of 84, 85, 108n
   see also Hinduism and Buddhism
Noah 10
nuclear family 15
Nurf Mirza Husayn Ali (Baha Allah) see also Baha'i 131
Nyaya 84

O

Occult 75, 77, 133, 143, 147
Oldham, J.M. 34
Old Testament 66, 71, 72, 78, 131
OPEC 69
Opium War 30
Ottoman (Turkish) Empire 31, 67, 68, 81n

P

Panikkar, R. 18, 23n
Pantheism 96, 144
Paraclete, Counsellor 66, 80
Parsee, meaning of 132

Parseeism, see Zoroastrianism
Paul 11, 22, 37, 53, 128, 135
Persecution 14, 26, 27, 29
    growth of Christianity under 27-29
Plato 108n
Polytheism 89, 96
Prayer 39, 41, 43, 44, 45,49, 53, 55, 78, 79, 97, 100, 113, 116, 118, 138, 149, 152, 153, 154
prejudice 14, 33, 38
proselytism 90, 136-7
    meaning and use of 137
psychedelic era *see* New Age movement
puja 21, 85, 88, 91
Purvamimamsa 84

Q

Qur'an (Koran) 21, 65, 66, 70, 72, 73, 74, 76, 77, 78
    on Christianity 72-3
    teachings of 71-3

R

Ramadan 72, 76
Rama Krishna (Sri) 89
Rama Krishna Mission 89
reincarnation, 21, 83-4, 85, 86, 89, 90, 91, 92, 96, 98, 133 *see also* Hinduism
relativism 9
religious groups population, countries/regions 163-170
    Africa 163-4
    Asia – East and South 166-168
    Asia – Indian subcontinent 166
    Europe – East (incl. Former USSR) 168-9
    Europe – West 168

　　　　Latin America and West Indies 169
　　　　South Pacific 169-170
　　　　West Asia, Arabia and Middle East 164-6
revelation of God 18-21, 60, 65, 66, 67, 72
righteousness 10
Roman, Roman Empire 14, 26, 28, 31
Roman law 26
Roy, Raja Rammohan 88
Russian Revolution 30

S

Sadhu Sundar Singh 88
Sai Baba 90, 142
Salvation 19, 21, 58, 84, 93-4, 96, 98, 100, 136
Samaria 12
sanatana dharma 94n
Sankya 84
Sathya Sai Baba 90
　　　healing 90
Sat Nam 95, 97, 98
Sayyid Ali Muhammad 131
Scriptures 17, 53, 55, 58, 137
Second World War 30, 31, 69, 118
Shamanism, 117
Shang Ti, *see* Confucianism
Shari'a *see* Islam
Shen, *see* Confucianism
Shintoism, Shamanism 117-9, 157
Shu Ching, *Book of History*, *see* Confucianism
Sikh, meaning of 96
　　　male, characteristics of 96

Sikhism 19, 88, 95-98
    on divinity 95
    suffering for faith 98
Smith, W. Cantwell 19
Socrates 108n
'Son of Man' 80
Spanish Civil War 1936 30
spiritual regimen 38
Sri Rama Krishna 88
statistics, global 157
    Christians 157
    other regions 157
St Francis of Assisi 67
super consciousness 144
surah 131

T

Taoism, Taoist 109, 111-12, 157
    meaning of 112
    symbol 112
    Yin and Yang, concept of 111-12
Theosophical Society 14
Theravada or Southern Buddhism 99, 100
Threlkeld, L. 130n
Triune God 21, 72-3, 80

U

underlying beliefs 60-61
uniqueness of Christ 48
United Bible Societies 34
Upanishads 83, 88

V

Vaiseshika 84
Vardhamana Mahavira (Jainism) 133
Vedanta 84
Vedas 83, 88
    on divine power 88
Vivekenanda 89
    on divine power 89

W

World Christian Encyclopaedia 170
World Congress of Faiths 89
World Council of Churches (WCC) 17
    Mission and Evangelism 17, 18
    Study group 1882 17
World history, some significant dates 158-162

Y

Yin and *Yang, see also* Taoism 111-12, 119
Yoga 84, 142

Z

Zen Buddhism 113, 118, 142
Zoroaster 132
Zoroastrianism, Zoroastrians 132-3
    Belief of deeds 133

about the author

Dr David Claydon has lived most of his life in cross-cultural contexts. He spent his childhood in the Middle East. Back in Australia he lived for seven years at the Anglican Hostel for Overseas University Students and spent some of the university vacations living with his hostel mates' families in Malaysia and Singapore.

After teaching economics for a year, he joined the staff of Scripture Union with responsibilities for its outreach program among high school students (ISCF) and to families in holiday resorts (CSSM/SU Family Missions). Later he was appointed SU's Associate Regional Secretary for East Asia and the Pacific and travelled extensively throughout the region training national staff.

During his time with SU he was awarded a Churchill Fellowship to undertake a cross-cultural study of how high school students formed their values in Singapore, England and the USA with a view to reflecting on the pressures to which Australian students were responding. He and his wife, Robyn then spent seven years in parish ministry, where they had the joy of seeing a parish grow in its commitment to mission, develop skills in local outreach and establish a parish-wide pastoral care network.

In 1988 David was appointed Federal Secretary of the Church Missionary Society of Australia (a voluntary Society within the Anglican Church, started in 1799). In this ministry he has spent three months of each year visiting national churches and CMS missionaries in various countries around the world.

David holds degrees in Economics and Theology and his doctorate is in the field of missiology. Ordained in the Anglican Church, he is a Canon of St Andrew's Cathedral, Sydney.